Are You Missing the Boat To Recovery?

How To Successfully Take Charge of Your Life

George W. Vroom

Health Communications, Inc.
Pompano Beach, Florida

WITHDRAWN

Dr. George W. Vroom
Priorities, P.C.
New York, New York

Cover design by Vicki Sommer

Library of Congress Cataloging-in-Publication Data

Vroom, George W., 1943-
    Are you missing the boat to recovery? : how to success-
fully take charge of your life / by George W. Vroom.
        p.   cm.
    ISBN 0-932194-63-X
    1. Co-dependence (Psychology) 2. Adult children of
    alcoholics-Alcohol use.   I. Title.
    RC569.5.C63V76   1988   87-26834
    616.86'1--dc19   CIP

©1988 George W. Vroom

ISBN 0-932194-63-X

Published by Health Communications, Inc.
                1721 Blount Road
                Pompano Beach, Florida 33069

*This book is
dedicated to the memory of my parents,
Margaret and George,
who never had the benefit
of the information contained
in this book.*

Acknowledgments

Of the many people who I am indebted to for help in writing this book I would like to single out for special thanks . . .

Michael Borecky, a professional colleague and valued friend, for not only his written contribution to the text but also for providing me with some of the basic knowledge about the disease of alcoholism, without which this book would not have been written.

Bruce Duff Hooten for his wisdom and spiritual guidance.

David Shay for his support and caring.

Michael Everett for his patience and kindness.

Sharon Wegscheider-Cruse and *Joe Cruse,* who as individuals and as a couple, continue to be a source of inspiration and hope for me.

And to all of the Adult Children of Alcoholics (ACoAs) who shared their lives with me.

Thank you.

Foreword
by Joseph R. Cruse, M.D.

Somebody needed to say it straight out, and George Vroom has said it. As a group, we health care professionals have "missed the boat" in our gate-keeping skills regarding alcoholism, other drug dependencies and the effects of the disease on the entire family unit.

Probably the most common affliction passing under the purview of such professions as medicine, nursing, psychiatry, psychology, social work, counseling and other therapy is being "missed". Part of the problem is that information regarding chemical dependency and co-dependency has rapidly accumulated and formed itself into a specific body of knowledge that is not yet fully disseminated or accepted. Universities and other training programs are resisting these new concepts outright or are just beginning to incorporate them into their curriculum.

The balance of the problem has largely been one of "I haven't missed the boat! I'm doing just fine in my work. So just don't rock *my* boat!"

Strange, we resist what we perceive we cannot control (treat, fix or cure) or what we fear (I may lose my patients or my credibility).

As a practicing gynecologist in the 1970s, I had to regularly learn new bodies of knowledge regarding concepts and techniques that evolved long after my formal training. I never gave it a second thought that I:

1. Needed to close my office,
2. Arrange for coverage,
3. Travel, and
4. Pay significant amounts of money for postgraduate workshops, training, education and certification of my abilities in such things as Cryosurgery, Laparoscopy and the use of the Laser in gynecology.

We, as health care professionals, need the same attitude toward developing our knowledge and skills in the areas of chemical dependency and co-dependency.

Health care professionals, in toto, must get on the next boat and become proficient in the diagnosis, treatment and referral, when needed, of this large cadre of patients who we are all seeing daily. Co-dependency and chemical dependency are treatable conditions and recovery rates run high. The satisfaction of participating in our patients' turn around and recovery is the caregiver's bottom line. It is energizing, gratifying and actually eye-opening for us.

George Vroom comes through by sharing his own therapeutic experiences. His caveat regarding "missing the boat" is prompted as much by his care and concern for misdiagnosed and untreated patients and clients as it is by his eagerness to share the joys of this kind of work with his colleagues.

The next boat is just leaving — don't miss it . . .

Joseph R. Cruse, MD
Onsite Training and Consulting
Rapid City, South Dakota

Contents

Introduction

This book owes its genesis to New York drama critic Clive Barnes. His review[1] of Pulitzer Prize winner Sam Shepard's autobiographical play, *The Curse of the Starving Class*, about a crazy family that symbolized "the decline, fall and dissolution of some mythic America of common dream", sparked my interest because I am a family therapist. Mr. Barnes said, "It is scarcely realistic — it makes the inhabitants of *Tobacco Road* seem like characters from *Peanuts* — yet its concerns are real enough, and its people have a certain likelihood to them. If cartoons, they are cartoons drawn from life." The review was replete with phrases such as "far-off symbols", "far-out metaphors" and "allegory runs riot like alligators in rainy season".

Determined to see this "classic American play" about the family, I rushed off on the last day and luckily got

---

[1]"Jukebox epics on a tuneless kazoo" *(New York Post,* June 1, 1985).

the last ticket to the last performance. After the curtain rose, I sat muttering through the whole performance variations of "I don't believe it!"

Certain likelihood? Cartoons? Baloney! Far from being "scarcely realistic", the play was a totally realistic portrait of an alcoholic family. On stage was exactly the kind of family that most of my patients came from. The "far-off symbols" and "far-out metaphors" were just like the real stories I listened to every week in my therapy groups for adults who had grown up in alcoholic families. The play was a garden variety Adult Children of Alcoholics (ACoA) story. (Sam Shepard is the eldest son of an alcoholic father, who was killed by a truck.) The brilliant 15-minute monologue by the eldest son about trembling in fear as his father, in a drunken rage, broke into the house while threatening to beat up his mother was an almost verbatim account of one that I had listened to the previous week in individual therapy from a Wall Street lawyer. Clive Barnes had "missed the boat".

Being an incorrigible chatterbox, I could not keep this information to myself and during the intermission I started talking to the stranger next to me in the theater. As fate would have it, the stranger turned out to be the play's producer, Patricia Daily. When I told her that the characters in the play were acting in the absolutely predictable pattern of all alcoholic families — a drunken unpredictable father, an enabling martyred mother, a caretaker hero eldest son and an acting-out scapegoat younger sibling — she was interested and agreed to come to my office to talk further. When she saw the clinical books on alcoholic family systems with descriptions and charts, she was astounded. She had absolutely no idea that the characters in the play were acting out a tragedy that was currently playing in millions of homes across the country. The producer had "missed the boat". She gave me a press packet, and I noticed that not one of the theater critics in the *New York Times*, *Time Magazine*, *The Daily News* or *Women's Wear Daily* had even talked about alcoholism, except very peripherally, and no one had seen this as a typical alcoholic family. They had all "missed the boat".

The "boat" they all failed to catch is the disease of alcoholism and its tragic impact on the American family. The disease is not "mythical" but very real and enormous. Not seeing it is like not seeing the ocean liner *"Titanic"* when it is sinking in front of your nose.

There are an estimated 14 million alcoholics in the United States, as well as another 56 million people affected by them. That is approximately one out of four Americans. Alcoholism is the direct or indirect cause of 95,000 deaths a year. The fatalities in the entire Vietnam War were 56,000. Accidents, homicides and homicides involving alcohol account for about 60,000 deaths a year. As a killer, alcoholism ranks third to cancer and heart disease according to The National Institute of Alcohol Abuse and Alcoholism (N.I.A.A.A.).

The Research Triangle Institute (RTI) estimates that the combined cost to the U.S. economy of Alcohol, Drug Abuse and Mental Illness (ADM) disorders was over $200 billion in 1984.

The impact of alcoholism on family members is also of *"Titanic"* proportions. There are an estimated 28 to 32 million adults in America who grew up in alcoholic families — like the one in the play that made "the inhabitants of *Tobacco Road* seem like characters from *Peanuts"*. A 1982 report from New York State treatment centers reported that one half of all alcoholics were adult children of alcoholics (ACoAs). It is far more than 50% in my experience.

The sons of alcoholic fathers are four times more likely to become alcoholics than the sons of non-alcoholic fathers, and the daughters of alcoholic mothers are three times more likely to become alcoholics than those women with non-alcoholic mothers. Daughters from alcoholic homes also tend to marry alcoholic men and produce more alcoholic children. So you can begin to see the magnitude and complexity of the problem.

In case you get confused and begin to think that my portrait of alcoholism and its impact on the family is "surreal" or exaggerated, it is important to go back to the basics. The basics in this case are a fundamental knowledge of alcoholism.

Alcoholism

Alcoholism is very real and very specific. The American Medical Association officially declared it a disease. A disease has specific causes, specific symptoms and is predictable within certain limits. Pulitzer Prize winner Lucinda Franks in a recent article on alcoholism[2], which she defines alcoholism as a disease in which the victim has lost control over drinking to the point where it interferes with his family and sound relationships or his job, states that "the myth that alcoholism is always psychologically caused is giving way to a realization that it is, in large measure, biologically determined."

The article talks about recent research in the area of blood chemistry, liver metabolism and brain waves in alcoholics and their offspring versus non-alcoholics. These tests show that while the disease may be set in motion by environmental and/or psychological factors, alcoholics fall prey to their illness because of their metabolism. They are genetically predisposed to alcoholism.

Alcoholism runs in families. People are basically born alcoholics. One could say it is like an "allergy" to alcohol — only it is not merely to alcohol but all of the benzodiazapines and barbiturates (families of sedatives which are cross-tolerant with alcohol). That means that alcoholics

---

[2]"A New Attack on Alcoholism" (*New York Times*, Magazine Section, October 20, 1985).

become addicted to Valium, Librium and all the other benzodiazapines. They also cannot use Doridon, Placidyl or any other sedatives. They cannot just have one. Not one!

Dr. Marc Schuckit of the University of California at San Diego, who is chief of alcoholism research at the Veterans Hospital in La Jolla, California, put it this way[3]: "This does not mean there's one gene and if you inherit it you become an alcoholic. But people do inherit things that make them more or less vulnerable to the effects of alcohol." He analogizes alcoholism to diabetes or hay fever.

As well as specific causes, there are specific symptoms of the disease of alcoholism, such as the blackouts — not pass-outs — and violent mood swings which were accurately demonstrated by the character of the alcoholic father in the play. There are also pseudo symptoms such as whether a person drinks at work or before noon or the amount a person drinks. There are false criteria usually used by drinking alcoholics to "prove to themselves that they are not alcoholics". The real disease of alcoholism is chronic and predictable — and as shown in the play — it always gets worse.

Co-dependency

Like alcoholism itself, people who grow up in alcoholic families exhibit certain specific unhealthy behaviors, share certain specific unhealthy attitudes and play certain specific unhealthy predictable roles in their work and love lives. This group of specific predictable symptoms is sometimes referred to as the "disease" of "co-dependency" or as "Adult Children of Alcoholics Syndrome". It is *not* genetically determined. *These common symptoms*

---

[3]Dr. Marc Schuckit, "Scientists Find Key Biological Causes of Alcoholism" (*New York Times,* August 14, 1984).

and behaviors are learned. They are the result of the common experience of growing up in an alcoholic family system.

Alcoholic family systems are dysfunctional in specific ways and are different from other types of family systems. The presenting problems of ACoAs are a direct result of adjusting on a daily basis in childhood to the specific kind of chaotic reality portrayed so well in *The Curse of the Starving Class*. The rules of the family system were originally established so that members of the family could adjust to having an active alcoholic as a member and still stay together. These roles and behaviors are survival mechanisms, functional adjustments to an unhealthy reality that continue long after their survival value is needed. They are an attempt by members of the family to bring order to chaos — but at a tremendous price.

In the play one can see the eldest son become a caretaker or hero in his struggle to save the family and the consequent pain it causes him. Because the hero role is already taken up in the family drama by the brother, the younger sister in the play becomes a scapegoat and gets in trouble. Again functionally speaking, her bizarre behavior is motivated by a need to save the family. There are other roles, and they are all functional.

Sharon Wegsheider explains in *Another Chance — Hope and Health for the Alcoholic Family* exactly how these roles work and their place in the overall alcoholic family system.

As Wayne Kritsberg points out in *Adult Children of Alcoholics Syndrome,* any person raised in an alcoholic family system, which has such characteristic rules of rigidity, silence and emotional isolation, will develop a set of characteristics similar to others who are raised in the same kind of system. His book charts out the four specific kinds of characteristics:

1. Emotional Characteristics, such as distrust and shame
2. Mental Characteristics, such as confusion and hypervigilance
3. Physical Characteristics, such as allergies and sexual dysfunction
4. Behavioral Characteristics, such as intimacy problems and inability to have fun.

What looks surreal — children acting like adults and adults acting like children — really makes sense if the system is understood as a whole. There are once again definite symptoms that can be traced to definite sources.

Two Separate Diseases

Thus, there are two separate distinct diseases which have different causes and symptoms. One, alcoholism, is a genetic predisposition toward becoming addicted to not only alcohol but all the benzodiazapines and/or the barbiturates. Bluntly put, those who are alcoholics "got the bad gene". They *must* stop drinking.

The other disease, called co-dependency or ACoA Syndrome, is a combination of attitudes, feelings and behaviors that are learned from living in an alcoholic family. Bluntly put once again, they can be unlearned.

Many, probably more than one half of ACoAs, have both diseases. If that is the case, then the alcoholism must be properly diagnosed and treated first. Then, *and only then,* can the co-dependency be looked at. If the therapist in charge understands all the variables, the patient gets better. If the therapist in charge does not know how to spot alcoholism or if the therapist looks at the patient's problems from an individual, rather than a systemic viewpoint, or ignores the role of alcohol in the whole system, then that person does not get better. The patient gets stuck, and because they are good ACoAs, they probably blame themselves. And those are the ACoAs already in therapy!

Denial

How could so many people, professionals and laymen "miss the boat" on what is the biggest family health problem in America? The answer, in a word, is denial. Denial is the chief symptom of both individual alcoholics and alcoholic families as a whole, even those who aren't alcoholic. It is very important to look at the role of denial in both diseases.

No drinking alcoholic will say he is an alcoholic. It is always his wife, the stress of his job, his horrible childhood (usually alcoholic) or the fact that he is a misunderstood genius. The booze increasingly comes between the victim and reality, and he is compelled to delude himself about his drinking. The alcoholic's family and friends often tend to look the other way when confronted with the symptoms, minimizing or rationalizing what they know to be true. Denial has nothing to do with intellect or not perceiving reality. It is emotional.

I remember talking to a very well-known writer, a public figure and public drunk, who cornered me at a social gathering to tell me about his problems, nodding his head in unconscious empathy while polishing off three double scotches as I described to him the basic symptoms of alcoholism, he said, "You mean, like F. Scott Fitzgerald." He agreed he did have some of those symptoms, but he felt that his drinking was not related to his problems. His problem was that he was in love with the maid.

Denial is present in the whole alcoholic family as well. They refuse to acknowledge to themselves the reality of alcohol's effect on the family or to see the connection between the alcoholism and their individual emotional problems.

The surreal quality, which shows up in the play, was brought home to me in another social situation when I brought a foreign visitor to dinner at a family of academics. Everyone was carrying on a conversation about Proust, no less, except the alcoholic parent who was babbling nonsense, while we made believe nothing was happening. Black was white, up was down and "everything was fine" — except for the person from outside the system, the "foreign guest", who took me aside to ask if our host was brain damaged.

"No," I told her, "he's just drunk."

"Then why is everyone making believe he isn't?" she asked.

"That's a very good question," I replied.

Denial is present in the mental health professional community as well. Unfortunately, as Lucinda Franks points out, alcoholism is so universally colored by social stigma that physicians tend to turn their backs on the situation. This is compounded by just plain ignorance about alcoholism in the whole mental health field. What professionals in the mental health field do not know about alcoholism could fill an encyclopedia.

I have spoken on numerous professional panels, institutes and conferences all over the country and when the question period comes, I have been appalled. These people do not know enough to know they don't know! Any recovering alcoholic who has gone to a few meetings of Alcoholics Anonymous knows more than these supposed experts. Whether it's as basic as you never give an alcoholic Valium, or that you cannot get an accurate diagnosis of any other psychological issue for three to six months after an alcoholic has been off liquor and pills, the therapists just don't know.

Unless the professionals have been exposed to an education on substance abuse or gone to self-help meetings themselves, then my experience has been that they do not have a clue as to what to do. Many of my patients have been to other therapists and are very angry at the profession in general.

The problem is ignorance rather than maliciousness or even conscious irresponsibility. Thus denial and ignorance combine to prolong the suffering of millions (1 out of 4 Americans) needlessly because these diseases are treatable. Alcoholics and adult children of alcoholics can lead happy healthy normal lives if they get the right treatment. One takes penicillin for an infection and chemotherapy for cancer! Over the years I've seen people get better and change their lives. In fact, with the right treatment, most people get better. If they do not get the right treatment, they get worse because alcoholism and co-dependency are progressive. It is less of a puzzle once one knows where all the specific pieces are. That is why proper diagnosis is especially important in this specific area.

Since alcoholism and co-dependency are specific "diseases", the information about them is *not* the missing link for all patients that are stuck in therapy and the techniques developed to treat them are *not* a cure-all for society's ills.

However, there are many men and women who grew up in alcoholic homes who suffer from depression, confusion about sexual identity, workaholism and most of all, disastrous relationships. They love too much, work too hard and never get what they want. And they are legion!

It is not understating the case to say that 30% of most therapists' caseloads are made up of such people. If untreated, the patterns in the family will continue. The rules and values will be internalized to be repeated in a new dysfunctional family. The "curse" will be continued — generation unto generation.

Purpose

What follows are the real stories of misdiagnosis and confusion that were experienced by real people. Some have figured out the puzzle, received the right treatment and got better. Some have not and have become worse. Some have died.

This book is written for those ACoAs who are still out there suffering, those who are confused and feel there is no hope. Some are just plain unhappy or anxious people who do not connect their problems to growing up in an alcoholic home. There are others who never thought of their parents as alcoholic. There are ACoAs who are also alcoholics, that are out there talking on psychoanalysts' couches about their dreams or their drunken mothers and still drinking. There are Jews out there who are alcoholics, who take Valium for stress, but do not realize that they are alcoholic because they believe the myth that "Jews can't be alcoholic". There are recovering alcoholics out there with 10 years' sobriety getting into an endless succession of terrible relationships because they deny that their alcoholic family of origin has affected them. There are many adult children of alcoholics, and even adult grandchildren of alcoholics who think they are hopeless neurotics who cannot change, just like their hopeless family situation could not change — because they are in the wrong treatment. They blame themselves. They do not realize that it is not because they have tried and failed again to solve their emotional predicaments, but that they have never addressed the issues properly. They feel like they somehow missed the boat. Well, they haven't. For all these people, there is hope.

Aside from an exposure of the misconceptions and mistakes that are commonly experienced by ACoAs who are trying to get help, I have included a section in each chapter on the correct diagnosis and "What is to be done", plus a chapter at the end on "What Works" which presents what I feel to be the basic necessary ingredients in any viable option for treatment.

My purpose is to demythologize and unconfuse the treatment field by making as much information available in plain English as I can, so that people can get help as quickly and easily as possible.

Each chapter represents a complex puzzle in which people were trapped, confused or duped by their families, professionals and themselves. Hopefully, you will find your story in one of the chapters and figure a way out of the maze.

_____Chapter One_____

First Things First — Double Trouble ACoAs

Alcoholism is a family disease. Everyone who grows up in an alcoholic family system is affected psychologically. However, because of the genetic predisposition factor, some children of alcoholics are themselves also alcoholics. Essentially they "inherit the bad genes". These ACoAs, using the terminology of the Introduction, have two diseases — alcoholism and co-dependency. Those ACoAs recovering from both diseases are referred to in the field of alcoholism treatment as "double winners". It is a conservative estimate, in my opinion, that over 50% of ACoAs are in "double trouble".

The reason why so many ACoAs are also alcoholic is simple. If there is alcoholism on one side of the family, for example, in your mother or her brothers and sisters, then your chances of being alcoholic are about 50/50. On the average, half the children of such a couple will be born with a genetic propensity towards alcoholism. That's an average, so for instance, in one family of four children, four might be alcoholic and in another family none might be alcoholic, but the average will be two. It's a matter of genetic roulette. But if there is alcoholism on both sides of the family, the percentage of alcoholics produced will be much higher.

Thus, the problems of the majority of ACoAs are compounded because they have two diseases. That's the bad news. The good news is that both diseases are treatable *but the alcoholism must be treated first.* If the alcoholism is not treated first, then any work on psychological family issues is ultimately worthless, and it is even counterproductive in some cases. The reasons for alcoholism being treated first are clinical and very specific. These reasons are also the source of many problems for ACoAs seeking professional treatment. Ignorant professionals, no matter what their degrees, often make the classic mistake of seeing alcoholism as a symptom, rather than as a primary cause of the patient's problems. They think that drinking is a symptom of unconscious conflicts stemming from early childhood and inadequate parenting. Once the underlying conflicts are resolved, they think that the patient won't need to drink or take pills. Nonsense!

Alcoholics do not take alcohol or pills to deal with the anxiety or depression that resulted from growing up in a mixed-up family. They get into trouble with alcohol and pills because they were born alcoholics.

As Dr. George Vaillant of Harvard, in his 40-year longitudinal study of 600 men says, "Those who developed alcoholism did not have prior problems. Instead, once the person lost control over alcohol, the problems began."

What prolongs the confusion in the misdiagnosis of the ACoA patient, who is also an alcoholic, is that once the false premise of the mixed-up childhood being the cause of present problems is in place, there is plenty of dysfunctional material from childhood to prop it up because all ACoAs are from alcoholic families, which are, almost by definition, mixed-up families. Every ACoA can tell you "crazy family stories" ad infinitum. During this process, which can go on for years, the therapist runs everything through this false analytic grid and does not see as particularly meaningful any information the patient might give about the real problem — alcoholism. The therapist never pursues any of those alcoholism areas because of ignorance, and in most cases, the patient never volunteers any information because of denial.

Results of Misdiagnosis

1. Without addressing the real causes of the alcoholism, the patient makes no significant progress in treatment. Instead of dealing with or "working through" any of the uncomfortable feelings arising from the therapeutic process, the patient medicates them with booze or pills. The patient never talks about it and the therapist never asks. As long as an alcoholic drinks or uses pills, then he is right back to square one. He cannot grow emotionally. Thus any alcoholic who is drinking or taking pills while in therapy is basically wasting his time, no matter how much insight he thinks he is getting. He is really getting worse because alcoholism is progressive.

2. Any drinking alcoholic who is in denial about his disease is only too happy to hear that the reason he drinks too much, if he even admits anything about drinking to the therapist, is because of his mother or his "crazy" family. To talk about these psychological problems makes him think uncon-

siously this is why he drinks. Thus the therapist unwittingly colludes in the patient's denial and helps the patient hide the real problem.

3. A drinking alcoholic can look like any number of clinical diagnoses. It is impossible to definitively tell what is going on in terms of underlying personality structure until the alcoholic has been off pills and alcohol from three to six months. I have seen alcoholics that look like narcissists. I have seen alcoholics that look like depressives or even manic-depressives, and I've seen alcoholics who act psychotic. Most of the time, much of that symptomology clears up when they stop drinking and go to treatment and/or join a self-help program, such as A.A.

Alcoholics from alcoholic family systems do have underlying psychological issues, which must be addressed. However, they cannot be looked at until the effect of alcohol and pills is factored out of the whole equation. In fact, when ACoA issues are dealt with too soon after an alcoholic ACoA has stopped drinking, it raises too much anxiety, feeds into the patient's denial, which is unconscious, and can result in the patient drinking again. Once that happens, then it's back to square one. Because once an alcoholic drinks, they have to deal with the alcoholism first.

The combination of the patient's denial and the therapist's ignorance is a classic combination which spells disaster for treatment. This cycle of misdiagnosis of "double trouble" ACoAs can go on for years, resulting in confusion and hopelessness.

What follows are several cases which illustrate how subtle and insidious the trap can be for alcoholic ACoAs. Despite these two patients' intelligence, education, and efforts, they were totally lost in the maze of treatment. In both cases the help came from outside their professional treatment. In both cases the patients had to diagnose their own alcoholism. The therapists never spotted it.

Greg

Greg is a 38-year-old alcoholic and a co-dependent. He is in "double trouble". He is an only child who grew up in an alcoholic home where his mother was the alcoholic. Like many alcoholics, his mother was flamboyant and unpredictable. She was a "good" and "bad" mother. She was the head of everything in their small town — the PTA, the Women's Club, the Junior League — but she also had increasing bouts of drinking and depression in which she asked Greg to save her. She did not ever admit she was an alcoholic, and eventually committed suicide.

Greg's father was typical of someone who marries and stays with an alcoholic, called a para-alcoholic in the alcohol treatment field. He was a rigid, hard-working businessman who saw himself as a martyr and showed little feeling. He held all his anger and hurt inside. He died of cancer. He was a classic "enabler". Greg's case illustrates how powerful denial is because he himself had a doctorate and post-doctoral degree in psychology, besides being a practicing therapist. He'd had some of the best education and training in psychology available — and he thought he knew about alcoholism. He'd heard about it all his life, in fact, the one thing his father had time and time again warned him about was becoming an alcoholic — like his mother.

When he came to me, he'd been in therapy for six years with three top therapists. Looking very intellectual in his tortoiseshell glasses and three-piece suit, he talked about his first therapist who he had seen twice a week for four years.

"It's hard to believe because she was so famous. She worked with Freud himself. She'd written books and lectured all over the country. I went twice a week for over three years, and we would talk about my girlfriend and our relationship. We would trace the patterns back to my relationship with my dramatic, beautiful mother who was not there for me. We would talk about insecurity and anxiety. Because I was a psychologist, we would talk about the individuation process and the work of Margaret Mahler, whom she knew. We would nail down in very precise terms the way in which my mother was an inadequate mother and how that resulted in certain patterns of neurotic behavior with my current girlfriend.

"We talked about fear of abandonment. We talked about how my father, even though he had been a successful executive, was probably unhappy in his work, and how that affected my attitudes towards work. We talked about me unconsciously not wanting to be more successful than he was — an Oedipal situation.

"We talked about existential *angst*, and the *angst* caused by me fooling around in the stock market. We talked about art, politics and philosophy. What we did not talk about was booze!

"I would say, every so often, that I thought I had a drinking problem. She would say not to worry about it because as soon as we resolved some of these conflicts about my mother, the urge to drink would go away. She said not to worry and I believed her. I realize now that was exactly what I wanted to hear. It's what every alcoholic wants to hear — their doctor telling them it's all right to keep drinking.

"I even remember one of the members of our therapy group getting furious because I had got drunk at a social gathering and divulged some personal information from group therapy which was totally inappropriate. Was she mad! She brought it up in a group therapy session, I apologized, and somehow it was glossed over. I remember feeling guilty far beyond what was called for. My doctor told me we ought to keep our eye on the drinking. However, it was gradually forgotten and displaced by other seemingly more significant topics — such as my girlfriend and my work.

"I felt stuck in therapy but figured she was an expert and knew what she was doing. It wasn't like I was making no progress in therapy. Besides, I liked her. I feel guilty in saying this but thank God she died, or I'd still be on her couch talking about my mother, while drinking and getting worse."

Greg knew, because his therapist had told him, that he had been diagnosed with anxiety neurosis. He was insecure and very anxious underneath an outgoing, expressive personality. His frantic overactivity and non-stop talking seemed a defense against being overwhelmed by anxiety. His dread of letting go and vague nameless fear fit all the classic patterns of an anxiety reaction. So did his love-hate conflict with his cross-sex parent (his mom) which Freud says is the unconscious cause for this behavior. Thus Greg and therapist #1 missed the boat. (Those are also classic symptoms of alcoholism which the therapist could have found out by attending any self-help group like A.A.)

After his therapist's death, Greg was still determined to get help. He did a lot of reading on his own and decided he was a narcissist. Besides, it was the thing to be in the late 1970s with pop books, television shows and everyone in the mental health community talking about it. So Greg went to one of the leading psychiatrists specializing in narcissism for a diagnosis — or rather a misdiagnosis.

Greg smiled as he said, "For two solid hours I did most of the talking, but he agreed wholeheartedly — I was a high-level functioning narcissist. I'd read all the books on narcissism and had mastered the highly complicated theory in this clinical area. Looking back on it reminds me of the 16th-century Pieter Breugel painting called *The*

Blind Leading The Blind. The bad news was that he told
me I would have to come three times a week at $100 a
session and I might make some progress after a few years.

   "I almost cried, I felt so hopeless. I could not afford
those fees, and it did not sound like a very good
prognosis. I still get mad when I think about it. That
stupid bastard! I was completely upfront about the
alcoholism in my family. In fact, I told him I wasn't sure
whether my father wasn't also an alcoholic. He should
have told me to go to A.A., which was free, and come
back to see him in a few months."

   Aside from making many of the same basic mistakes
that this first therapist made, the new "expert" just got
fooled by the symptoms of alcoholism in a more
sophisticated way.

   Narcissism is a character disorder which comes from a
particular kind of bad parenting done very early in
childhood development. It leaves the person unable to
empathize with other people in a very basic way. They
cannot get out of themselves. Narcissists are characterized by an air of grandiosity which pervades their
personality. This grandiosity covers an orb of feelings of
depression and low self-esteem. I had a patient with a
real narcissistic character disorder: after two years of
therapy, he would still come late almost every session
and not understand that I had to end the session on time.
He was a busy lawyer! Everyone in group therapy hated
him because he thought he was a "big deal". He just did
not "get" therapy and finally quit. That is a narcissistic
personality disorder. True clinical narcissists are extremely difficult, self-centered patients and they change
very slowly.

   Drinking alcoholics display many of these same
symptoms on the surface. Many are grandiose, self-
centered and try to be big shots. There is an A.A. saying,
"Everyone builds castles in the sky, but alcoholics tend
to move in." Underneath they are scared, depressed,
resentful and have a low self-image — even if they are

successful. They feel like a piece of garbage at the center of the universe.

F. Scott Fitzgerald is the quintessential "alcoholic personality", idealizing the "rich" and at the same time always feeling like an outsider. However, in the case of the alcoholic, these symptoms are caused and maintained by use of the drug alcohol. Alcohol is a sedative which depresses the brain. Years of using this sedative daily and living in a drug world is going to cause the user to live more and more in his own dreams. These delusions are grandiose to compensate for his increasing depression and inability to deal with reality. Alcoholics retreat to the dream world more and more as the disease and use of the drug progresses. These similar symptoms are *not* due to "improper mirroring" from Mom at the age of three years old. Anyone from any family will begin to feel that way if they drink enough.

The big difference is that alcoholics get better if they stop drinking and using pills. They get better rather quickly and dramatically in my experience. Clinical narcissists do not.

Of course, after the alcoholics deal with the alcoholism, they must still deal with the co-dependent issues if they are from an alcoholic family, but that is getting ahead of our story.

Scared but undaunted, Greg continued his search for a new therapist. This time he found a doctor who was the head of the psychiatric department of a major New York hospital who Greg felt was also a "nice guy".

About this time Greg switched medical doctors and went for a physical exam. His new doctor took a family history, and because the new doctor had done an internship at an inpatient alcohol rehabilitation hospital, he told Greg that he probably was an alcoholic. High blood pressure, fatty liver, alcoholism in the family, not remembering things while drinking (blackouts) and daily drinking over the last few years were symptoms of the disease of alcoholism. The new doctor, a cardiologist and internist, was able to diagnose Greg while the psychiatrists weren't because he knew the right questions to ask. Greg said he heard the reproach of his dead father in his ears, "I never want you to become an alcoholic," but the new M.D. had presented facts of alcoholism being a disease in a very professional, non-judgmental way. Greg believed him and started going to Alcoholics Anonymous.

Greg shook his head and smiled ironically as he told me what happend at the third psychiatrist's office when he talked about alcohol to his new therapist.

"He said it was fine to go to A.A., but he was not enthusiastic and felt that it was not central to my problem. 'You are always talking about alcohol. What are you, obsessed? We really must focus on these issues about your mother.' His psychiatrist said, 'You have an alcohol phobia. You think because your mother was an alcoholic and your father could have been, that you are an alcoholic also.' When I asked him if he was aware of the American Medical Association's statistics on the genetic odds of being an alcoholic from my kind of a family, he admitted he was not. I was beginning to suspect this guy did not know even the basics about alcoholism that I was learning at A.A. This was confirmed when he said, 'You are not an alcoholic like those other alcoholics — you are a psychologist, a doctor.' I told him that was just the point. I was just like those other alcoholics, and if I thought I was different or special, people in A.A. said I would never get better. In fact, I told him if he kept it in professional confidence, I would tell him a secret. The speaker at the A.A. meeting the night before was his colleague, the famous brain surgeon at his hospital. Yes, indeed, doctors and psychologists could also be alcoholics! Then I quit."

Greg stuck with A.A. and got himself a sponsor. If he had come to me in this period of his recovery, I would have focused almost entirely on his alcoholism and made sure he was working the A.A. program and speaking up at meetings. I might have put him in an early sobriety group with other recently recovered alcoholics. But the focus in individual therapy or group would not be on early childhood issues or his "mom". For reasons mentioned earlier in this chapter, going into the issues this early in Greg's recovery would be counter-productive.

The alcoholic, ACoA or not, has to become aware at this point he does not have several problems of which drinking is one. He has one problem — drinking! Early sobriety therapy is highly structured and the therapist must be directive. *The therapy must contain participation in a self-help program, such as Alcoholics Anonymous.* This goes against the training and philosophy of many therapists. They don't like telling people what to do and most do not really know what actually goes on at A.A.

It is only after the early sobriety issues are dealt with in the double-trouble ACoA that the psychological issues can be addressed. Since recovery from alcoholism is a process that takes time, and I believe there is no substitute for time, these psychological issues that are normally thought of as the guts of therapy should be gradually introduced into therapy anywhere from six months on — depending on the individual.

In Greg's case, his timing is generally on target. He used his two years in A.A. to get a solid grasp on the issues surrounding the alcoholism. Since he had stopped drinking, he said his general anxiety was down, he felt he had matured quite a bit and had more confidence in himself. He felt more at home in his own skin. He told a funny story about therapist #3 who he had inadvertently run into at a therapists' conference.

"He came up to me and said I looked great. And he asked what had happened. I told him about A.A. and my feelings about myself. Then he said something few people have ever heard any psychiatrist say, and I quote, 'You were right and I was wrong!' He said he would send me patients with alcohol problems and he did.

Greg must continue in A.A., but now he is ready to address the issues which come out of his growing up in an alcoholic family — his second disease!

Sally

Sally's story is not too different. She is a 32-year-old very attractive young woman, and is from a family in which her mother and father are both alcoholics. But they are rich alcoholics. That means they can prop up their denial by covering up their mistakes outside the family with money or firing confronting therapists. Her two younger brothers both have drinking problems and have been in numerous car accidents and financial difficulties — always to be bailed out by "good old Pop". Mom was a sullen drunk, a martyr and a victim. Sally, the eldest daughter, is a super-achiever and after graduating at the top of her class in the "best" schools, she becomes a partner in one of the "best" New York law firms and has a list of accomplishments a mile long.

Eight years ago she went into psychoanalysis with one of the "best" psychiatrists in New York. She had gone because of her compulsive workaholism and her disastrous relationships with men, in which the men she fell in love with were always inaccessible. She told me that she had been diagnosed as a narcissist — which was this doctor's specialty. Two years ago, she found out, on her own, that she was an alcoholic. That's six years after starting three times a week therapy! I asked her what she talked about in all those sessions for six years.

"We talked about my father who is a rather romantic figure and a local hero in our state. But he also beat me up when he was drunk, as well as my brothers and my mother. Our home was always in turmoil, between his extra-marital affairs, my parents fighting and the boys getting in trouble. High Drama! So there was always plenty to talk about, especially my love-hate relationship to my father."

She had gone to A.A. on her own but didn't receive much encouragement or comment one way or the other from her doctor. When I asked her why she had come to me, she said that she'd gone to a few Adult Children of Alcoholics' self-help meetings and things seemed to make sense there for the first time. Someone there had told her about me and she was curious about alcoholic family systems. She was thinking of quitting her job, and was living with a guy who she was not happy with. She felt she had made some progress in therapy but she felt she had missed something someplace. She was stuck in therapy but felt she had invested so much, so long and with such a "famous" doctor that she was really in a quandary about what to do.

What to Do

If you grew up in a home with one or two alcoholic parents and you want to avoid the pitfalls and confusion that befell Greg and Sally, the place to start is with yourself.

If you are an ACoA and have ever had any issues with booze or pills, or question in your mind as to whether you are alcoholic or chemically dependent, *then assume you are, rather than that you are not.* Next, conduct an investigation to prove or disprove that assumption by using real criteria.

Some of the real criteria used by the National Council on Alcoholism are based on a combination of physical, behavioral, mental and attitudinal signs which are found during the early, middle and late phase of the destructive drinking process. These are not the "phoney" tests used by drinking alcoholics. They are not based on hearsay but on scientific fact gathering.

Criteria For The Diagnosis Of Alcoholism

BEHAVIORAL

1. Direct Effects

Early:

Gulping drinks
Secretive drinking
Morning drinking

Middle:

Repeated conscious attempts at abstinence

Late:

Blatant indiscriminate use of alcohol
Skid Row or equivalent social level

2. Indirect Effects

Early:

Medical excuses from work for a variety of reasons
Shifting from one alcoholic beverage to another
Preference for drinking companions, bars and
   taverns
Loss of interest in activities not directly associated
   with drinking

Late:

Chooses employment that facilitates drinking
Frequent automobile accidents
History of family members undergoing psychiatric
   treatment; school and behavioral problems in
   children
Frequent change of residence for poorly defined
   reasons

Anxiety-relieving mechanisms, such as telephone calls inappropriate in time, distance, person or motive (telephonitis)

Outbursts of rage and suicidal gestures while drinking

PSYCHOLOGICAL AND ATTITUDINAL

1. Direct Effects

Early:

When talking freely, makes frequent reference to drinking alcohol, people being "bombed", stoned, etc., or admits drinking more than peer group.

Middle:

Drinking to relieve anger, insomia, fatigue, depression, social discomfort

Late:

Psychological symptoms consistent with permanent organic brain syndrome

2. Indirect Effects

Early:

Unexplained changes in family, social and business relationships; complaints about spouse, job and friends

Altered or impaired work performance, frequent job changes, financial difficulties

Spouse makes complaints about drinking behavior, reported by patient or spouse

Major family disruptions; separation, divorce, threats of divorce

Late:

Job loss (due to increasing interpersonal difficul-
ties)
Overt expression of more regressive defense mech-
anisms; denial, projection, etc.
Resentment, jealousy, paranoid attitudes
Symptoms of depression; isolation, crying, suicidal
preoccupation
Feelings that "I am losing my mind"

As you proceed with your investigation, realize that if
you are an alcoholic, denial will be working full time to
say "That's not me" — "Yes, but I . . ." There are some
direct questions that the National Council on Alcoholism
have prepared for people to diagnose their drinking
behavior. They are simple *yes* or *no* answers. If you are
an ACoA with "double trouble", you will be tempted to
"fudge" the answers. Try to be honest. Yes or No!

1. Do you occasionally drink heavily after a disappointment, a quarrel or when the boss gives you a
   hard time?
2. When you have trouble or feel under pressure, do
   you drink more than usual?
3. Have you noticed that you are able to handle more
   liquor than you did when you were first drinking?
4. Did you ever wake up on the "morning after" and
   discover that you could not remember part of the
   evening before, even though your friends tell you
   that you did not "pass out"?
5. When drinking with other people, do you try to
   have a few drinks when others will not know it?
6. Are there certain occasions when you feel uncomfortable if alcohol is not available?
7. Have you recently noticed that when you begin
   drinking you are in more of a hurry to get the first
   drink than you used to be?

8. Do you sometimes feel a little guilty about your drinking?
9. Are you secretly irritated when your family or friends discuss your drinking?
10. Have you recently noticed an increase in the frequency of your memory "blackouts"?
11. Do you often find that you wish to continue drinking after your friends say they have had enough?
12. Do you usually have a reason for the occasions when you drink heavily?
13. When you are sober, do you often regret things you have done or said while drinking?
14. Have you tried switching brands or following different plans for controlling your drinking?
15. Have you often failed to keep the promises you have made to yourself about controlling or cutting down on your drinking?
16. Have you ever tried to control your drinking by making a change in jobs or moving to a new location?
17. Do you try to avoid family or close friends while you are drinking?
18. Are you having an increasing number of financial and work problems?
19. Do more people seem to be treating you unfairly without good reason?
20. Do you eat very little or irregularly when you are drinking?
21. Do you sometimes have the "shakes" in the morning and find that it helps to have a little drink?
22. Have you recently noticed that you cannot drink as much as you once did?
23. Do you sometimes stay drunk for several days at a time?
24. Do you sometimes feel very depressed and wonder whether life is worth living?

25. Sometimes after periods of drinking, do you see or hear things that aren't there?
26. Do you get terribly frightened after you have been drinking heavily?

If you have answered *Yes* to any of the questions, you have some of the symptoms that may indicate alcoholism. That alone does not make you an alcoholic. Yes answers to several of the questions indicate the following stage of alcoholism:

Questions 1-8 = Early Stage
Questions 9-21 = Middle Stage
Questions 22-26 = The Beginning of
the Final Stage

Bluntly put, if you are an ACoA and you hit a couple of *Yes* questions here and there — you are in trouble. You should then proceed to the next step in your investigation.

Go to a few A.A. meetings and see if you can identify with the feelings or attitudes of the speakers. The meetings are free; they never hurt anyone. No one is going to call you an alcoholic, and at least you'll get a look from the inside at what your parents felt like while they were drinking. You can also attend ACoA self-help meetings, but that will not directly address the question of whether you are an alcoholic.

After attending 10 or more A.A. meetings and reading as much as you can on the disease from such clinically accurate books as *Under the Influence* by Dr. James R. Milam and Katherine Ketcham, then I would seek professional help.

When interviewing therapists, or if you are an ACoA already in therapy, I would make sure my therapist knew something about alcoholism. You should not ask him if he has dealt with alcoholics or you will get the same answer as Greg and Sally did, which is "Why, of course" and sometimes they add, "and I always send them to A.A." That doesn't mean they know anything about alcoholism or how A.A. or Al-Anon or ACoA works.

Ask them, "How many A.A. or Al-Anon meetings have you ever attended?" Or ask them specific basic facts about alcoholism that you've learned from your reading or attendance at A.A. meetings. If you are not satisfied with their answers, I would walk out and go to someone who does know. If you are already in therapy and you like your therapist, make sure that he does go to a few meetings, reads a few books and learns about the disease. It's the least he can do. Remember, you're the consumer. You're paying the bill, so you're entitled to not be misdiagnosed or maltreated.

If after your personal investigation, you are sure you are not an alcoholic, count yourself lucky and proceed to address your ACoA issues. If you are an alcoholic as well as an ACoA, then be realistic and no matter what emotional or financial crises are happening in your life, address the alcoholism issue first. That means not hiding or confusing the issue by going to Al-Anon and ACoA meetings before going strictly to A.A. meetings. Probably going to 90 meetings in 90 days and getting a sponsor is a good start. That means saying to your therapist, "I'm an alcoholic and I need to focus primarily on this issue for the next three to six months. Can you help me?"

A.A. works. Most people who follow their suggestions get and stay sober. People who try to run their own recovery program get into trouble. Ask for help, listen to what others say and leave "doing it my way" to Frank Sinatra! If A.A. and out-patient care are not enough, then you might need in-patient care at one of the many good in-patient rehabilitation programs. This is nothing to be ashamed of. The point is to get sober so you can become a "double winner".

The road to understanding your alcoholic family, if you are also an alcoholic yourself, starts here and keeps "first things first".

_____ Chapter Two _____

Physican,
Heal Thyself

Since so many people in any alcoholic family system have a genetic propensity to get addicted to not only alcohol, but also to the benzodiazepines and the barbiturates, I have included a chapter on a special kind of misdiagnosis — physicians who, out of ignorance, denial or both, hand out these pills to alcoholics. If a doctor himself has a problem with alcohol or pills, of course he will be in denial and deny the destructive effects of handing out pills to his patients.

Giving an alcoholic any of these drugs is like giving him a drink. If the alcoholic is drinking, he will invariably abuse them, and if he is trying to stay sober, it will act like "the first drink" and eventually lead him back to drinking.

For ACoAs who are also alcoholics, as described in Chapter 1, this additional factor can make the maze of treatment even more complicated because it is the psychiatrist himself who is causing the problem by prescribing the drugs. The ACoA in double-trouble is only doing what the psychiatrist told him to. He wonders why his problems do not go away, or why they get worse, but he trusts his doctor and keeps going to him to talk about his childhood issues and get "medicine". Of course, as you know by now, that alcoholic ACoA is getting worse because his disease is progressing below the surface. He is getting "dry drinks" from his doctor!

An ACoA, who is also an alcoholic, is likely to run into this particular kind of maltreatment at two different points in his recovery from both diseases. (At both points, the result is utter disaster for the patient!)

The first point is when both diseases are active, in other words, when he just knows he has "problems", is still drinking and goes to a doctor for help for depression or "nerves". Sometimes he might go to a psychiatrist who does not know how to ask the right questions to find out if he is an alcoholic or a psychiatrist who does not know that alcoholics can't take certain pills, and prescribes them as part of the treatment.

Sometimes an ACoA/alcoholic might just go to his family doctor, not a psychiatrist, because he feels he has temporary problems with his wife or job and needs "a few Valium to get through a rough period". The family doctor, because he wants to be helpful or "a nice guy" — and is ignorant about the disease *or hasn't taken a sufficient family history when he started treating the patient to find out if there is alcoholism in the family* — gives out a prescription to the patient.

The patient invariably abuses the prescription. He also never sees his problems as his own or mental but as a function of his environment. In denial about his own alcoholism, he says to himself, "Everyone takes a little Valium to get through the stresses of living in the modern world. They're not addictive. What's the matter with that?" There's lots the matter if you are an alcoholic.

The scenario of the "well-meaning" family doctor takes place more often than you think, especially if the ACoA/alcoholic seems to be functioning well in society — in other words, if he is a "solid citizen" with a wife, kids and a job, rather than an "alcoholic bum". Most ACoA/alcoholics fit the former rather than the latter description — for a while!

The second point in the recovery continum that may cause trouble for ACoA/alcoholics is after they have addressed their alcoholism but not their co-dependency. For instance, they might already be sober in a self-help organization, such as AA, but still experience anxiety or depression arising from unresolved ACoA issues activated by a relationship that doesn't work out or a disappointment at work. In other words, their second disease kicks up its heels.

At this point, the person might work the AA program to the best of his ability, talk to family and friends but the anxiety or depression does not seem to go away. He then might seek professional help from a psychiatrist who is ignorant, or in denial, about what alcoholism really is. The doctor might give the patient pills and tell him not to worry. I've seen cases where the patient has said that they cannot take Valium or Xanex because they are alcoholics and the doctor has told them that it's "nonsense" or "AA is a cult which is against all pills".

Once the patient starts to take any of these pills, which he is in reality "allergic" to, all hell breaks loose. It is just like drinking. He activates the first disease, gets more depressed or anxious, mixes up the issues of the stress rising from his alcoholism and those generated by his co-dependency, and often goes back to drinking.

At best he is confused. At worst, he is dead! I've included several cases of this kind of misdiagnosis to illustrate how in real life, with the best of intentions, people can be misled and hurt. The first case is one where the patient is just beginning recovery.

Jim

Jim is a handsome, funny 26-year-old actor who lives in Soho. He is an alcoholic, from an alcoholic family and has a long history of abusing not only alcohol but Valium, Librium and any other drug he could get his hands or nose on. He had been to A.A. a few times and didn't like it. However, someone there had recommended a psychiatrist he might call if he needed advice on stopping drinking. He has subsequently learned about pills as well as alcohol and tells the story this way.

"I had not been using pills for a while, but I'd been drinking very heavily, in fact, around the clock for days. My body finally couldn't take it any more. I called up the shrink for an appointment and by the time I got to his office, I was a mess. I was shaking, crying and said 'I'm an alcoholic'. He agreed and asked if I wanted to go away to treatment. I said no so he told me to go to A.A., and he gave me a prescription for 10 Restorils (a benzodiazepine) of 5 milligrams each — those are the yellow ones.

"So I went to A.A., back to work, and came to see him once a week during which time we talked about my family, especially about my relationship to my father. He never asked about A.A., and he never asked me about any pill abuse in the past. Never once!

"After a week or so, I realize now, I started to get hooked on the Restorils. So the third meeting I got a larger prescription from him of 25 yellows (5 milligram) Restorils. After about three weeks, I lied when he asked me what color Restoril I was taking. I said blues because I know they were 10 milligrams each. So then I got a 50-pill supply with refills on the prescription from him. That is 150 blues, which is 1500 milligrams of Valium — up from the original 50 milligrams which were 10 yellows. Oh yes, I also talked a pharmacist I met at a party into selling me 50 more blues. I was taking them as needed! That worked out to at least 50 or 60 milligrams a day.

"The shrink never asked me once about them. In fact, I also lied and told him I could not sleep. So he gave me 15 (30 milligram) Dalmanes — another benzodiazapene — to help me sleep. I had enough pills so that I was stoned all the time. I figured I was not drinking so I could take all the pills I wanted to. It wasn't until about 60 days after I stopped drinking that my sponsor in A.A. warned me against the pills. I guess I got scared because I flushed them down the toilet and went cold turkey.

"It was a little rough for a few days — jumps and fidgets — but I got through it. When I finally told the psychiatrist that I felt I had been getting addicted to the pills and decided to give them up, he said 'fine' and showed no reaction. The icing on the cake, though, is his reaction when I told him I'd been sober for 90 days in A.A. He said, 'Well, you're not an alcoholic any more.' "

Wrong, Doc! Dead wrong! Luckily, by this time Jim knew enough about his disease to know the doctor had "missed the boat". He called him up and said he would not need to see him anymore, but he never told him why. Jim went to a doctor who did know about alcoholism and today he is just fine.

Ellen

Ellen is a 44-year-old Florida suburban housewife who is an alcoholic and has been in A.A. for just over 10 years. Her father, a businessman and "trouble" in his day, is also an alcoholic, age 66, and has been in A.A. for 14 years. She has a son, Bert, age 19, who after a few embarrassing episodes of drinking at college, has just started to go to A.A. meetings, but is not yet convinced he is an alcoholic. Ellen's husband, Brian, age 46, is divorced, charming, financially successful in real estate, and still loves to "party" and chase women. He has never quite "grown-up". If I had to bet, I'd put money down that Brian probably "is", rather than "is not", an alcoholic, since daughters of alcoholic fathers tend to marry alcoholics and he surely acts like one. So one could safely say that Ellen and her family have been exposed to the disease of alcoholism and also have some knowledge of what works and what doesn't.

Yet when her daughter, Jennifer, went off to college and started getting depressed and complaining about missing home, her condition was never connected to the "family" disease of alcoholism. She was drinking at college but, she said, no more than anyone else, and she stated emphatically, "I'm certainly not an outrageous drunk like Bert!"

Instead, at the husband's insistence, and because he was paying the bills, she was sent to the "best" psychiatrist in town. He prescribed Xanax which he said was a new "wonder drug" that fought both anxiety and depression at the same time and was non-addictive. Jennifer's depression improved for a while but then she started to get mood swings and vague feelings of being lost, and discontent with her life returned.

Ellen was in a quandary about her daughter and was referred to me by telephone. I told her that there was a good chance her daughter was an alcoholic and that Xanax was a benzodiazepine and thus "trouble". She brought that information to her daughter's psychiatrist, who insisted that it was safe and that her daughter needed it for her depression. This was backed up by her husband, who supported the doctor both verbally and financially.

The girl kept drinking "like everyone else", even though the doctor had warned her not to mix booze and sedatives. They are dangerous because they are synergistic [2 + 2 = 5]. The result was that she got into a huge accident while driving in a Xanax "blackout"! Fortunately, she was not seriously hurt although the car was "totaled".

This brought the family to their senses. Ellen fought for and got a consultation about her daughter with a second psychiatrist, this time a "famous" doctor who was a real expert in the field of alcoholism. He recommended another psychiatrist. The husband listened to him, and the daughter is now on the road to recovery.

John

John, a 63-year-old senior executive with a large corporation, was not so lucky. His six figure income and material success did not help him. He was an alcoholic and ACoA who had been in A.A. for 11 years. His wife came to me for a consultation because he was suffering from bouts of debilitating and excruciating depression. He was a success and everyone loved him. But he felt awful about himself. She said he went to A.A., and he also had been going to a psychiatrist for four years. There didn't seem to be any improvement in his condition. Nothing seemed to help. She or he didn't know what was wrong. I asked if he had been tested for manic depression [basically a salt imbalance which needs to be treated with lithium — another salt], and she said he had been tested and was not a manic depressive. I said the whole story did not make sense and asked her to bring him in to see me. She left, and I did not see her or her husband for five years.

Then I ran into her in the street and the missing pieces of the puzzle fell into place. He had remained miserable and in addition had got cancer. He had died recently. On his deathbed, he had confessed that he had lied. He had not stayed sober all those 11 years in A.A. but every six months or so went on a secret "bender". That is not a sober alcoholic but a "periodic" alcoholic who has never stopped drinking and is kidding himself. Then I asked her if the psychiatrist had given him any pills. Yes, she said without knowing what she was saying, the doctor had prescribed Valium all along because of John's high pressure international job. Suddenly it all made sense. I realized John never had a chance, even if he had wanted to stay sober. The doctor was giving him dry drinks every time he went for help.

In all of these cases, the real help came from the outside and intervened in an already existing system of pseudo-care. For John, it never came at all. Unfortunately, the more the patient believes and does not question the system of misdiagnosis and maltreatment, the more difficult it is to extricate himself and the worse he gets.

The Good Guys

Fortunately there are responsible concerned M.D.s around who are aware of the disease of alcoholism and its ramifications for ACoAs. They are not only aware of the need for education about these diseases among the general population, but also aware of the need for education among their own profession. They are also willing to speak out about the current abuse and misdiagnosis in the field.

One such person is Michael Borecky, M.D., a graduate of Columbia University College of Physicians and Surgeons who is on the staff of a major New York hospital and has done consulting work for several inpatient rehabilitation centers for alcoholism. He is not a psychiatrist but an aware physician whose specialty is internal medicine. I think it would be helpful to let him speak for himself.

"I take care of patients with a wide variety of medical conditions in an office in New York City. I have acquired skills in treating drug dependency during the past 15 years. What started out as a moonlighting job as a medical resident in a drug rehabilitation unit has become a subspecialty in my practice. I see active alcoholics and recovering alcoholics. I take care of their medical problems. A significant portion of my time with these patients is spent helping them avoid prescription drugs given to them by other physicians.

Dr. Borecky's Patients

"Mark is an ACoA who had been in Alcoholics Anonymous for 5 years. As an opera singer, Mark had used alcohol 'to further my career. I always had loved to drink on social occasions. Then I found it helped stop my shaking when I auditioned. After I landed the chorus job at the opera, I found I needed a drink to get on stage. I was found to have low blood sugar.' (Alcohol can cause the blood sugar to drop precipitously.) 'Soon I needed a drink to be able to leave the house. I fell on my fanny during a performance and realized I was an alcoholic. That was when I went to A.A.'

"Mark was sober and enjoying middle age when his doctor detected diabetes. The fact that Mark was overweight and on 'water pills' for high blood pressure (both can elevate the blood sugar) was ignored by the physician. A diabetes pill was given to lower Mark's blood sugar.

"Soon Mark started having the same symptoms of low blood sugar (also called hypoglycemia) that he used to have back in his drinking days. His doctor increased the dose of medication and the symptoms got worse. Obviously the diabetes was being 'overtreated' by using the drug — rather than by using effective, yet milder, modalities, such as diet and changing to a different kind of blood pressure medicine that wouldn't affect the blood sugar.

"Instead of realizing his error, Mark's doctor prescribed a sedative drug called Ativan to 'calm his nerves'. Having learned about sedative-hypnotic drugs in A.A.,

Mark told his doctor that he was an alcoholic and could not take any 'mood-changers'. The physician reassured him that this drug was not like the others. He said it was perfectly safe and did not cause addiction. Mark started taking the Ativan and immediately felt better. Mark was referred to me by a friend in A.A. who told him that Ativan might not be a safe drug for him to take.

"The sceptical A.A. friend was absolutely correct. Ativan is a member of a class of drugs called benzodiazepines. These are sedative-hypnotic drugs also known as 'minor tranquilizers'. They have been sold in this country since the 1960s. The most notorious of this class are Valium and Librium. They are looked on by most doctors as being quite benign. This is because they are not seen in successful intentional suicides-by-overdose. Before the introduction of benzodiazepines, the medical profession had been plagued by deaths from people overdosing on popular sedatives of those times, such as barbiturates, meprobamate (Equanil), glutethimide (Doriden), ethchlorvynol (Placidyl), methyprylon (Noludar) and ethinamate (Valmid). Alcoholics, by the way, are also 'allergic' to these drugs.

"Benzodiazepines are commonly prescribed for 'anxiety states', 'insomnia', 'tension states', and 'depressive symptoms'. They are included in the general class of sedative-hypnotics. *But what not everyone realizes is that the leading non-prescription, 'over-the-counter' drug of this group is alcohol.*

"Therefore, all the members of this group — in fact, all the drugs named thus far — are cross-addictive (that is to say, if you're addicted to one, you are addicted to them all). Giving a recovering alcoholic this drug is like giving him or her a drink of alcohol. Taking a benzodiazepine put Mark in grave danger of becoming addicted to Ativan and/or returning to alcohol.

"Fortunately, the dose Mark was taking of the Ativan was not yet high enough for him to be in danger of having a withdrawal seizure if the drug was abruptly stopped. Therefore, he did not require a detoxification. We stopped the Ativan immediately. However, Mark had to experience withdrawal symptoms of irritability, nausea, insomnia, trembling and palpitations, lasting for two weeks. He also had to overcome fears of leaving the apartment and fears of being public (unique features of his addictive pattern) all over again through the help of his A.A. friends.

"We also stopped the diabetes pill and the blood pressure pill and worked on weight reduction and a healthier diet and eating pattern. Since then the diabetes has been controlled in this way.

"Mark's doctor was the type that I call 'heavy-handed' or 'fast on the draw'. Like the heroes of the Old West (and probably wishing to be as commanding a figure to their patients), they 'write prescriptions first and ask questions later'. They may mean well, but they over-prescribe medication without thinking about side effects. If in addition they are uninformed about sedative-hypnotics and about drug addiction, they can cause tremendous suffering to active and recovering alcoholics.

Physician's Desk Reference

"In the 1987 *Physician's Desk Reference (PDR)* over 12 different benzodiazepines are listed (there are actually 15 in use). In the description section of Ativan doctors are warned, 'Anxiety or tension associated with the stress of everyday life usually does not require treatment with an anxiolytic [drug].' (Anxiolytic is another name for a minor tranquilizer.) In their self-treatment programs in A.A. (which may or may not include individual or group counseling sessions with a counselor or therapist knowledgeable in drug addiction), recovering alcoholics learn to cope with everyday anxieties and stresses without the use of the mood-altering drugs that they are addicted to. As they continue in recovery, they discover that they can survive even unusually stressful events without the aid of mood-altering drugs.

"A few years ago I was called by distressed A.A. members regarding a colleague whose husband had died suddenly. They felt that her distraught condition required the use of sedatives. I asked to speak to the bereaved widow, and I offered to give her a small supply of a sedative — but I asked her if she really felt she wanted to take it to 'alter her mood' of overwhelming loss. This mood, as she and I discussed on the phone, was really quite appropriate to what had happened in her life at this time. She was experiencing real grief due to a real cause. She replied that she wanted to experience the death of her beloved spouse without drugs because it was in fact 'part of life'. She thought she could do it by herself with A.A. and with friends. She did it and feels good about it to this day when she comes into the office.

"Everyday stress can easily become severe stress for recovering alcoholics and adult children of alcoholics who have not learned about ways of handling stress that don't involve drugs or co-dependency. Physicians need to acquire more respect for the tremendous psychological power of mood-altering prescription drugs, and for these drugs' insidious ability to addict susceptible patients. Once these drugs are introduced as part of the coping mechanism that alcoholic or co-dependent patients use to deal with everyday life (assuming that we all realize and agree that everyday life can in effect be quite stressful), it becomes very difficult for these patients to live without these drugs.

"The drugs, in fact, are advertised as something that will make your life easier to deal with. For an alcoholic and for some co-dependent persons, sedative-hypnotics become a sort of charm bracelet or ancient talisman that people believe they must have with them in order to survive in life.

"Of the benzodiazepines, the fifteen listed by the New York State Department of Health (sheet RX-95) are:

Chemical or Technical Designation	Drug Company Trade Name
Alprazolam	Xanax
Chlordiazepoxide	Librium
Clobazam	Frisium
Clonazepam	Clonopin
Clorazepate	Tranxene
Diazepam	Valium
Flurazepam	Dalmane
Halazepam	Paxipam
Lorazepam	Ativan
Midazolam	Versed
Nitrazepam	Mogadon
Oxazepam	Serax
Prazepam	Centrax
Temazepam	Restoril
Triazolam	Halcion

"Time and time again in covering other physicians' practices — during a weekend, for example — I will get an urgent call that so-and-so 'has run out of Tranxene that he takes every four hours and he has to keep taking it and must have a refill'. What condition could he possibly have that would require him to take a minor tranquilizer on a chronic basis? There is simply no such condition! Chronic anxiety states require counseling and therapy. The track record for sedative-hypnotic drugs in treating this kind of condition is terrible. If the person being treated in this way has a drug dependency, then the outcome may be life-threatening.

Labels

"Fortunately, as of July 1, 1987, prescribing benzodiazepines in New York State requires a triplicate prescription form and requires that the drug container be labeled *"Controlled Substance, Dangerous Unless Used As Directed"*. A copy of the prescription is then filed by the pharmacist with the New York State Bureau of Controlled Substances. This, it is hoped, will make doctors more aware of the potency of the benzodiazepines, and may help the state to identify physicians who have a tendency to overprescribe these potentially addicting medications.

"However, there are still many sedative-hypnotics available (including the older and in some ways more lethal ones that we mentioned earlier), that don't require special prescriptions and labeling.

"Also it is difficult for the state to keep an eye on every practitioner. Therefore, A.A. members and ACoAs will have to continue to hold their doctors accountable for the side-effects of every drug prescribed. They should also hold themselves accountable for every drug they buy over the counter, and ask their physician or pharmacist what it contains. To try to increase their safety in an environment teeming with 'mood-changers', they will have to continue to share their concerns about drugs their physicians have prescribed for them because sometimes these physicians can be uninformed.

"It is easy to be seduced by clever labeling in a culture dominated by slick advertising. How many of us have heard a TV sports announcer chiming: 'This Bud's for you!' when an athlete hits a home run? Would the drug he is selling sound as seemingly harmless and benign if he shouted to the player: 'This fermented ethanol's for you?' Likewise it is easy to forget what the facts are with the minor tranquilizers. The drug company trade-name "Ativan" makes the drug sound like an old, respected friend. Would Ativan sound quite so noble and traditional if the doctor referred to it by its chemical name, Lorazepam?

"In my opinion, one of the few worthwhile uses of these drugs is for short-term sedation for agitated anxiety states. An example would be a patient who is in a pre-operative state in the hospital facing an operation the next morning, and who can't sleep the night before. However, when used on a chronic basis, these drugs, like alcohol, are nothing but trouble."

What To Do

What to do to avoid these pitfalls again starts with you. If you are an ACoA, you should, as Dr. Borecky suggests, hold yourself accountable for every drug you buy across the counter. That means getting educated about the different drugs and just what they do. Read and talk to your doctor. It also means that if you are already in treatment and taking *any* drugs, ask your physician if they are benzodiazepines or other sedatives that might be addictive if you are from an alcoholic family. It might even mean finding out what drugs members of your family are taking and "passing the word on" about the possible changes of those sedatives to them. They might have absolutely no idea.

As Dr. Borecky also said, physicians should also be held accountable for what they dispense. The best way to help make them accountable is to give them all the information they need to make a proper diagnosis by giving them a full family medical history, which includes everything about pill and alcohol abuse in your family for as far back as you can go. If you are an alcoholic ACoA, it should be on your medical record in case of medical emergencies or hospitalizations. There are choices of what pain-killers to give in hospitals. If you are alcoholic and your doctor knows, then he can advise the attending physicians what not to use.

I've heard many terrible accounts of recovering alcoholic women who have gone into the hospital to deliver a baby, only to return with a "postpartum depression" which turns into drinking because they've been given Demerol. They or their doctors never connect the drug with the depression. Often they don't know they have been given the drugs, and their doctors do not know they are alcoholics.

So go to your family doctor or to your psychiatrist if you are already in treatment with one, and tell him about any alcoholism or pill addiction in your family tree. If you are not sure, read the next chapter and learn how to do a genogram and find out if there are any. Ask family members for information and then sit down with your doctor and talk. *The main point is that if there is alcoholism in your family, do not be ashamed about it.* It is a disease, like heart disease or cancer, which runs in your family, and he is a doctor. Both he and you deserve to know.

_____ Chapter Three _____

All in the Family

Many ACoAs have a problem seeing the alcoholism in their families, sometimes even after they have identified themselves as alcoholics. Because of the "denial" of all the members of an alcoholic family, or the "denial" within the larger "family" of a cultural community or an ethnic group, they usually will not see the alcoholism or pill abuse as such. In addition, family members certainly will not see it as part of a larger pattern. Thus, there is no reinforcement from the ACoA's family for this particular issue. In most cases, there is disbelief or defensive alternative explanations about the behavior of various family members.

Thus, the individual and his family fail to see the reasons for family members' problems having anything to do with alcohol or pills. If this failure to see is reinforced by a therapist, who out of ignorance or denial, fails to diagnose the alcoholism in the whole family system, then the problem is compounded. An inadequate, and thus inaccurate, picture of the patient's family emerges. This false family portrait can cause trouble for treatment of ACoAs in several areas.

If the person is alcoholic as well as an ACoA, not recognizing the alcoholism in the family system may help bolster the person's "denial" about his own alcoholism if he is still drinking. If they have stopped drinking, or are not alcoholics in the first place, it can prevent them from getting help for their co-dependency — such as happens to the people in Chapter 4. If they are non-alcoholic ACoAs who want to get help, it can prevent them from getting the proper help such as is the case in Chapter 5.

If I do a proper multi-generational diagnosis, with a genogram, of an alcoholic family, I can always find patterns of alcohol and pill abuse. These patterns not only make sense, but they change the way I look at the case and thus, the way I do therapy.

What follows are the cases of several people who are in various stages of recovery from either one or both diseases — alcoholism and co-dependency. In all cases, knowing the family pattern of alcoholism and pill abuse changed the treatment considerably. One case was my mistake, which I later corrected. Two others found the right treatment after wasting years in the wrong treatment, and the fourth is a tragedy which is going on as I write this book.

Tim

Tim is a 30-year-old computer programmer who is the third child in a family of six children. He was originally from Indiana. He is not alcoholic, and was sent to me by the Manager of the Employee Assistance Program (E.A.P.) at his corporation because he was depressed and having problems with his supervisor. He complained about being underappreciated and underutilized. He did not like his boss, and, in addition, he was having problems with his girlfriend. And he was also very serious. In fact, he demonstrated almost all of the characteristics that Janet Woititz talks about in her book *Home Away From Home* — dedicated to Adult Children of Alcoholics in the workplace.

However, Tim came through my door several years ago, before the book was written and while I was just learning about alcoholic family systems. So at first I saw Tim as a typical depressive. He came from a large family with high expectations and not enough love and re-affirmation of each child to go around. Individuals from such families never can come up to their own internalized, unrealistically high expectations and are continually depressed. Their self-worth comes from not who they are but what they achieve. And it is never enough!

Tim's father, now retired, had worked his whole life in the steel mills and sent all his kids to college. He said his mother was overweight and always had problems with depression. Since his elder brother and sister were 10 years older, he had to "pitch in extra" to help raise the younger kids. There were plenty of reasons to feel angry and gypped in Tim's family.

So, at first, I diagnosed and treated him from the perspective of psychoanalytically oriented psychotherapy — as an individual. From that perspective, the main task is to get the patient to express the anger that he could not, or never learned to, express as a child. This is what underlies and causes the depression. That's all well and good — as far as it goes. But it really left a lot of questions unanswered in Tim's family.

One such question was why the absolute fury in Tim's father, which would every so often break out from his usual quiet martyr pose, and show itself through physical violence. Another was Tim's emotionally distant picture of his mother and some of his consequent problems with his girlfriend. More subtle questions revolving around

Tim's being very out of touch with his feelings, as well as distortions in his self-image, also were a puzzle to me.

Some of his attitudes corresponded to attitudes that I was currently reading about in the Adult Children of Alcoholics literature. He sounded like an ACoA but I did not want to jump to conclusions. What I did do was to begin to change the way I approached the case and ask different questions.

The first clue was that Tim said his eldest brother had gone through three wives and might have a drinking problem. When asked about the younger three he had "raised" and to whom he was especially attached, he admitted that he was worried about one and maybe even a second having drug and drinking problems.

During the next session, I asked more about his mother's chronic depression. He said she stayed in bed "a lot". When I asked what "a lot" meant, he said sometimes for days. When I asked if she took anything for her depression, he said Valium. Lots of Valium! Then I knew — Mom was an alcoholic who took Valium and was still active.

Suddenly things began making sense because I had begun to ask the right questions. Dad's rage and martyrdom were typical for a person who stays married to an alcoholic and does not go to Al-Anon. Tim's attitudes were right on target for the hero or eldest child in an alcoholic family. Tim was the eldest child in the "second" family, since his elder siblings were so much older. His need to achieve, frustrated expectations and depression now had an additional context. All "heroes", such as the son in *The Curse of the Starving Class,* feel the need to achieve in order to bring the family together or "make it all right". Of course, they cannot because the only thing that will make the family all right is for the alcoholic to stop drinking, which the "hero" cannot do. Thus, under a hardworking, compliant exterior, the hero often feels inadequate (no matter what he does, it never changes), guilty (maybe he has not done enough) and he invariably feels frustrated and very angry (because he keeps trying and nothing changes). This explained a lot of the problems at work.

The discovery of alcoholism in Tim's family also explains quite a bit in regard to his almost obsessive attachment to a woman who was emotionally inaccessible to him and had no realistic intention of changing. He was going to "save" or "rescue" her, so she could love him. This is a recurring pattern in the love relationships of Adult Children of Alcoholics.

The additional analytic grid of the alcoholic family system allowed me to see the case differently. It not only provided me with new information, but also gave me an additional context from which to view the case. It explained many of Tim's unconscious attitudes and projections which were being played out in his love life as well as at the workplace. It also explained Tim's being out of touch with his feelings and his "protecting" all the members of his family.

The real payoff in regard to this shift of focus on my part was for Tim in his therapy. In addition to applying this additional system's grid to individual therapy, I also put Tim into an ongoing group I formed at that time, composed entirely of Adult Children of Alcoholics.

In this group, the focus was on the feelings experienced growing up in an alcoholic family and, in some ways, the group actually became a new healthy family in which honesty and feelings were respected. Tim also started going to ACoA self-help meetings.

After the change in approach, Tim's progress in therapy was incredible. Far from being fired, he left the original job of his own accord to go to another company with a 50% raise in salary. He left his girlfriend and found another one, whom he married. They bought a house in the country and had a baby. Oh yes, he's not depressed any more — and he has been out of therapy for two years.

Gail

Gail is a 42-year-old artist from Houston, who is a recovering alcoholic — 12 years sober in A.A. She had been divorced from her first husband, who was an alcoholic, for ten years. The issue she had been struggling with twice a week over the last three years, with one of the country's leading psychoanalysts, was her relationship to men.

She had grown up as an only child from a "privileged background". She described her mother as rich, powerful and tough — she'd inherited a fortune from the oil business. She said her father was weak and had been emasculated by her mother. He had worked in the oil business until he was about 50 years old then because of "company politics", he had "retired" to "write and live off his wife's money". He was "brilliant" and a "gentleman", and even though he became increasingly depressed after he had retired, he was a "humanist who always had time for people". It was obvious that she identified with him more than with her mother.

In her psychoanalysis, the psychiatrist had focused on her relationship to her "weak" father and her relationship to her "strong" mother. In brief, she picked weak men like her father and then tried to control them like her mother. Much of the time was spent analyzing the nuances of successive relationships she had had with men in her past. The analyst was extremely nondirective and much of the time was spent analyzing the unconscious sexual and aggressive feelings she had towards men. She felt she had "resolved" some of her issues and "understood" the complicated three-year relationship with the guy she'd broken up with a year ago. She was now "in love" with a 29-year-old poet, whom she'd met in A.A. six months before.

While visiting New York City, she came to me for a consultation on the recommendation of a friend who said I specialized in alcoholism, because she felt that she had been over the same ground once before in analysis — and the relationship with the poet was falling apart dramatically. She said she did not understand why she was acting the way she was toward the young man.

This time I was ready! The first question that I asked her after I heard her story was, "If you are an alcoholic, who's the alcoholic parent in your family?"

"There aren't any," she replied.

"What did your father take for his depression as he increasingly 'retired' to his writing studio?" I asked.

"Valium!" she said.

Then I knew it was not just a matter of a "rich bitch" mother and bad luck in the oil industry. Alcoholics do not become alcoholics overnight. Thus her father's career disaster and his failure to fulfill his "brilliant" potential did not happen overnight. They were the manifestations of a progressive disease of attitude. While she was growing up as a child in her alcoholic family, her father's increasing emotional withdrawal and alcoholic attitudes had influenced her mother and the whole family system more than any of the other seemingly significant causes. Her mother's attitudes and behavior could be explained as the emotional reaction to living with an alcoholic, as well as by being brought up "spoiled" or "secretly hating men".

As for Gail's relationship to men, I pointed out that all her close relationships to men in the past, including her husband, were with alcoholics — a fact that had somehow escaped her psychiatrist. Daughters of alcoholic men tend to "fall in love" with alcoholic men, even if the alcoholism is in its earliest stages and no one would ever guess the men were alcoholics by their drinking behavior. This is because of an unconscious identification on the daughter's part with her father, both as the first "big man" in her life, like every little girl does, but also as a "victim of life" who valiantly tries hard and often has a dramatic or romantic style. Children of alcoholics usually identify with the alcoholic, rather than the para-alcoholic mate.

I then asked another question that had never come up in her analysis. "How long has your young poet been in A.A.?"

"Six months," came the reply.

"Gail, you know if you've been sober in A.A. for 12 years that six months is not very sober and that no one in A.A. is supposed to have an involved romantic relationship for the first year. So it's doomed from the start."

She burst into tears, "I know but he's so good looking!"

"But also unstable, dramatic, 12 years younger than you and not really there for you. There is no chance this could ever work. I hate to be so blunt, but — get rid of him!" said I.

As mentioned before, ACoAs are notorious for picking inaccessible partners in love relationships. However, often they are "blind" to their potential lovers inaccessibility. The "new" ones are different from the "old" ones who did not work out, and somehow the ACoAs are bound and determined, because they "love" the latest one, that the new relationship is going to work out. The ACoAs often need guidance and direction in their folly, rather than an intellectual analysis with no direction.

After two sessions, Gail returned to Texas where she not only got rid of her young poet but her famous analyst, too. She got herself a therapist who knew something about alcoholic family systems. When I talked to her the last time, she'd been with the new ACoA therapist for about a year and felt she was making progress. For the first time in years, she did not have a boyfriend and was focusing on her own emotional life.

The Jewish Conspiracy

The ACoA issue of not being able to see the alcoholism in your own family takes place on the grandest scale in a huge family of sorts — the Jewish community. The

Jewish conspiracy is a conspiracy of Jewish people against themselves. There is a "myth", passed on by Jews about Jews, that Jews cannot be alcoholics. That is simply not true. They can be crazy or "meshuggener", and they can have emotional problems [in fact Jews have always taken leadership roles within the mental health community, starting with Sigmund Freud himself], but alcoholics they cannot be! That is for the "Wasps", the "Irish" or maybe even the "Poles". Besides, "everybody knows that Jews do not drink — never did!" So goes a theme, or variations of it, that hurts untold numbers of alcoholics and ACoAs, who may be drinking or using pills, and who happen to be Jewish.

In fact, what is especially insidious about the circumstances around these particular cases is that the alcoholic may never touch alcohol but abuse pills instead — one of the benzodiazepines or barbiturates.

"How could a person be an alcoholic and never touch alcohol?" many people ask. Well, if you've read this book so far, you know that because these drugs are cross-tolerant with alcohol, not only can you be an alcoholic and use these "dry drinks" instead, but that you will demonstrate the same attitudes, behaviors and progression that someone who drinks does.

One patient of mine, Morton, was an executive in the garment industry, a stressful occupation by any measure, and never drank except for an occasional drink at family gatherings or a glass of wine on religious occasions. Once, only once, he had an incident where he got out of control but basically he did not like alcohol — it made him feel woozy and out of control almost immediately — so he stayed away from it. But he inhaled Valium to deal with the anxiety of his job.

He started to get mood swings and depression, which got worse over the years, and went to a total of five different kinds of therapists — he even got Rolfed — without any success. It was a chance conversation with a friend in A.A. that got him to me, where we began to get him sober.

What makes it extra difficult to see the pattern of pill or alcohol abuse in your family if you are Jewish is if it is pill abuse rather than alcohol abuse, if the pills were prescribed by the doctor, if there's a tolerance within the family for both mental health problems and therapy answers, and in addition, there is just no word within your community to describe what is wrong with you — then it's always got to be described in other terms. You'd have to be bloody Sherlock Holmes to realize you're an alcoholic. To illustrate the extent of the problem and the seriousness of the damage it does to peoples' lives, I've taken one family and re-examined it, using the new knowledge that there is alcoholism in the family. The reason this new knowledge came about is because of the recovery of one of the family members from both alcoholism and co-dependency. The rest of the family is still out there suffering — in "denial".

So here is Ruth Rapp's story as told by her daughter, Deborah, who is a 40-year-old investment banker and an A.A. member for eight years. Deborah has a younger brother, Jack, who is not an alcoholic.

Ruth Rapp

"My father, Charlie, had a drinking problem but everyone, except him, recognized it for what it was after a while. Besides, he was a Wasp and my mother's family, the Rapps, half-expected it because Wasps all drink too much. With my father, at least I had a warning before 'the bomb' hit because I saw him go and pour himself a drink. But with Mom it was more terrifying because with pills I never knew. Suddenly, she turned into another person. Out of nowhere she became an angry screaming witch who hit us. It was awful. It started in the early 1950s when she was abusing Placidyl, Seconal, Tuanol and some other barbiturates. During this period she had several suicide attempts on pills, and she was in and out of psychiatric wards. [See Dr. Borecky's comments on barbiturate abuse and the switch to benzodiazepines during this period in Chapter 2.] Things just got worse.

"Then in the early 1960s Mom got a new psychiatrist who recommended some new drugs that had just come on the market. I remember the names because this new shrink put her on a "drug diet" — two Clonopin every four hours, one Restoril every two hours, a Halcion in the morning, and Dalmane to sleep. It was a disaster! I realize now they were all benzodiazepines and, of course, she abused them all. And all roads lead to alcohol. She started drinking with the pills so that by the late 1960s she'd overdosed several times on pills and booze.

"At this time she divorced my father and married another alcoholic — but a Jewish alcoholic. He was something else! He'd had two liver operations from undiagnosed alcoholism, and by the time she met him, he said he wasn't an alcoholic because he only drank Campari and soda and that wasn't really drinking!

"Anyway Mom was mostly into Valium at this time, around 1975, and on one of her many overdose trips to the hospital, she finally ran into an M.D. who knew what he was doing. He diagnosed her as an alcoholic, sent her to the hospital's 30-day program for alcohol rehabilitation (which she completed) and told her to go to A.A. But her second husband, 'Big Irv', as I used to call him, forbade her to go to A.A. meetings. I can hear him now: 'That is absolute nonsense, Ruth. You couldn't be an alcoholic. You are Jewish!'

"From that time on, her addiction went underground. She is a closet pill taker. She still takes Valium and Dalmane, goes to a shrink and is desperately unhappy. The added tragedy is that last year she got cancer so she'll probably never get sober. She is 65 years old and has been in and out of shrinks' offices since she's been 19 years old — that's 46 years — and nowhere, except for that M.D. at the hospital, was she diagnosed as an alcoholic."

In terms of Ruth's own family of origins the Rapps' understanding of her, they said that Ruth has problems because she was adopted [translate that as she's really not a blood member of our family which, as you will see, is not true], or she has emotional problems because of the stress of her childhood [the pill problems are seen as being generated by childhood conflicts and thus should be addressed by therapy] or Ruth drinks because she married Charlie and he drinks [a combination of moral reproach where Ruth deserves to pay for her bad judgment in choosing a marriage partner and the general idea that bad habits like drinking are infectious].

All the family explanations, aside from not recognizing Ruth's problem as a disease, also put the problem outside the family as though it had absolutely nothing to do with the Rapp family. A realistic look at the facts, through the use of a genogram, shows that quite the opposite is the case. The Rapp family is loaded with alcoholics. However, as Deborah says, there is some kind of underlying premise that We are God's chosen people, so it couldn't happen to us.

What Is To Be Done

To find out whether you have any hidden alcoholism or pill abuse in your family will take some work. You must talk to all the members of your family as far back as you can to find out information. Assume they are going to be in "denial" so do not ask if "Uncle So-and-So" was an "alcoholic" or a "pill freak". They might turn up as "eccentric" or "a wild man", or "he became very withdrawn in his later years", or some of the explanations you have seen in this chapter. Don't make relatives defensive, but if you "smell blood" then pursue with very factual questioning such as "What did he do after that?" "Was she ever drunk?" or "What medicine did Granddad take?"

If you do enough research, and if there is alcoholism in your family, a pattern will emerge. Then you can put that down on paper in the form of a family genogram. The more you work with the family genogram and perhaps ask more questions of your family to fill in the blanks, the clearer the pattern will become. You will discover new things about your family that you didn't know before. You will realize that certain members of your family have been mislabeled. You will find alcoholics hidden behind bushes, such as old maiden aunts that nobody has talked about for 50 years. Suddenly things will start to make sense.

Let us take Deborah's mom's family — the Rapps — as an example. Ruth grew up in the home of Jessica and Jacob Rapp. Jacob came over from Russia as a young man and built a fortune in real estate in New York in the Twenties. He was known as a "womanizer" and "a wild man" among the family, but he was discreet about it. He would disappear with his girlfriend for several days at a time, but his wife would "tolerate" it and said nothing to anyone outside the family because he was a good provider.

Jessica was known as a controlling manipulative woman, who was a martyr for her children. A "Jewish mother" par excellence but also a "para-alcoholic" par excellence. They had a daughter, Sophie, who at 15 years old had a child, Ruth, out of wedlock with a man we'll call "Mr. X," who had a drinking problem. The illegitimate child Ruth was kept and raised by her grandparents, Jacob and Jessica, pretending that her mother Sophie was her sister.

Sophie got married at age 22 to a man named David and they had two children — a boy named Jesse and a girl named Jane. Jesse, now in his fifties, is an alcoholic, although financially successful. Jane, also in her fifties, has had a lifelong problems with barbiturates and

Valium. She is married to the child of an alcoholic, Arnie.

Jacob and Jessica also sired two other boys — Abe, two years younger than Sophie, and Jason, four years younger than Sophie. Both boys, now in their sixties, are alcoholics — one had a successful business career but was a closet drinker his whole life, and the other has had "pill" problems his whole life because of the "depression caused by him never being a real success like his brother". Sophie, the only non-alcoholic offspring of Jessica and Jacob, "fell in love" with an alcoholic "Mr. X" and produced an alcoholic child, Ruth, who in turn married two alcoholics in succession and mothered an alcoholic child — Deborah. When this information is put in genogram form, you can see a pattern. On the following page is a partial genogram of Deborah's mother's family. The alcoholics or pill abusers have been circled.

When looked at this way, it is obvious that old patriarch Jacob probably was an alcoholic also. What was he doing on those three-day disappearances with his girlfriend? His sons, Abe and Jason, get the bad alcoholic genes but his daughter Sophie doesn't. However, like most daughters with alcoholic fathers, she is attracted to alcoholic men. As a teenager, she acts out and has a child with one. For Ruth, Deborah's mother, who has alcoholism on both sides of her family tree, the "genetic cards are stacked against her" in terms of being an alcoholic. Sophie, Ruth's mom, is carrying some of Jacob's bad genes as shown by the fact that when she does marry a non-alcoholic man, David, she still sires two alcoholic children, Jane and Jesse. Ruth, Sophie's alcoholic daughter, keeps marrying alcoholics and has an alcoholic daughter, Deborah. The only bright spot in the current generation is that Jack is not an alcoholic and of course, that Deborah is recovered. Nobody in the family, aside from her, sees themselves as alcoholic. So much for the non-alcoholic Rapps!

The point is that it takes some knowledge of the disease of alcoholism, lots of hard work and most of all perseverance to cut through the tangle of family denial in order to get at the truth. Even if you can't do anything about changing your family, at least you will know what the truth is, and as Deborah said in my office after doing this genogram, "I just feel lighter."

The Rapps

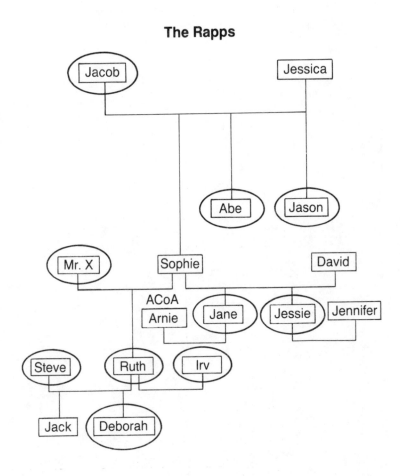

_____Chapter Four_____

Stuck

There are many ACoAs, who are also alcoholics, who have dealt with their alcoholism by going to a self-help program such as Alcoholics Anonymous and/or therapy, but are in denial about their second disease — co-dependency. They refuse to see the connection between their present emotional problems and their alcoholic dysfunctional family of origin. Their boat to recovery has run aground. They are stuck!

There are many ways that these people misdiagnose their own problems and suffer needlessly. There are many stories that they tell themselves and believe, so that they can prevent themselves from getting the help they need. Sometimes these stories that the individuals tell themselves make sense to only them, and sometimes they find other people to prop up their version of reality, but at base, like most forms of denial, they are telling themselves lies. Underneath, these people are scared.

They are scared of their own feelings — the pain, anger and shame of growing up in an alcoholic family. Here are a few of the stories.

"A.A. Doesn't Work — For Anyone"

This fiction can take many forms but it usually happens during the first few years of recovery after an ACoA, who is also an alcoholic, has dealt with many of the immediate problems resulting from alcoholism. After a few years in A.A., he has his health, his family and some good friends back. If he has lost his job, he probably has a new one, and most of all, he has regained some semblance of sanity himself. He has regained the basics but he may be running into problems in his love life or his work life.

At first, he was enthusiastic about A.A., and had "great expectations". However, now he is probably running into disappointments in terms of his expectations about his relationships (either in getting along with his spouse, or in finding a suitable "healthy" partner) and his expectations about himself at work. The disappointments and frustrations he is running into are the same feelings that ACoAs who are not alcoholics run into because of their dysfunctional alcoholic family background.

He is angry, guilty, frustrated and feels all the other innumerable negative emotions that other ACoAs experience. And because he is no longer sedating these feelings with alcohol or pills, he probably feels doubly overwhelmed by them. He then takes some of this anger and projects it onto A.A.

I've had more than a few people say, "A.A. helped for a while, but it was the same old stuff. All they talked about was alcohol, and all my sponsor told me to do was keep working the A.A. steps. My depression did not go away, and I worked the A.A. steps all the time. After a few years I lost interest." These people are running right into the symptoms of their second disease, with which A.A. does not claim to deal. A.A. only claims to deal with alcoholism!

Another variation on this "disillusionment with the A.A. program" takes the form of saying that A.A. is a cult or a religious organization and is in some way morally reprehensible.

One patient, Charlie, had been dry for 11 years but had not been to A.A. for six years. Charlie had been sent to me by a knowledgeable Employee Assistance Program (E.A.P.) manager at his job, who knew about Charlie's terrible alcoholic family background. Charlie came to the E.A.P. complaining about severe headaches and chronic depression. Charlie felt that A.A. was really out of line with his conservative Christian fundamentalist church views on issues regarding sex and politics. When I pointed out that A.A. did not have any views on sex, politics or anything else, except that alcoholics could not drink, he jumped into a million theological reasons why he had stopped going.

Thank goodness, his emotional pain was acute enough at the time so that he stayed in therapy and can now see his theological gymnastics as a defense not to feel the pain of his frightening and confusing childhood in an alcoholic home. After a year of therapy, he agrees that as soon as he starts talking about something abstract or starts taking moral stands on "great issues", he really is on the run from his feelings. He has returned to A.A. and likes it. He has put the theoretical questions about God and the Universe "on the shelf" for a while. He sees the spiritual part of A.A. as "practical" rather than religious. He feels more comfortable and has more emotional security in order to tackle some very painful family issues.

"A.A. Doesn't Work — For Me"

This form of denial is particularly sad for some individuals. They believe in the A.A. program, participate in it fully and yet because of underlying ACoA problems, they feel that they are different. They become emotionally more and more isolated and gradually drop out.

There is one line at the beginning of Chapter 5 of A.A.'s "Big Book", *Alcoholics Anonymous,* that says: "Rarely have we seen a person fail who has thoroughly followed our path. Those who do not recover are people who cannot or will not completely give themselves to this simple program, usually men and women who are constitutionally incapable of being honest with themselves. There are such unfortunates. They are not at fault; they seem to have been born that way."[4] They focus on that paragraph. They become convinced that they are that one rare person.

One young woman, a secretary, age 34, named Kathy, who finally got to therapy because she was dragged in by her A.A. sponsor after an unsuccessful suicide attempt, explained the feelings this way. She had been in A.A. two years.

"I had a terrible time talking at meetings. I would go and sit in the back. After the meeting, I would try and socialize but I'm not much at small talk. I held all my feelings in. I went to a small meeting for over a year and felt I still was not part of the inner circle of people there. I was always on the outside. I knew it wasn't their fault. I always blamed myself. I didn't drink but I was miserable. I felt I was one of those people they talked about in 'the Big Book' who was constitutionally incapable of getting the A.A. program. I've just always felt like a loser my whole life, why not this, too. I had no

---

[4]*Alcoholics Anonymous* (A.A. World Service, 1939), p.58.

boyfriends, and I disliked my job. I even began to feel I was 'crazy'. I had no hope. I figured 'what's the use'. That's why I tried to kill myself."

Kathy wasn't crazy. She was angry and scared and believed it would always be that way. She had grown up in an alcoholic home as the family scapegoat, where her mother and sisters treated her like the family "screw-up". She just couldn't do anything right in their eyes, even though she had worked her way through college and her sisters hadn't. Her inner scapegoat role was out of sync with the reality of her achievements.

Her alcoholic father had beaten her mercilessly since age 5 for reasons she could not to this day figure out. To add insult to injury, five years ago her father had got into A.A., retired to Florida with his wife and they both had totally "blocked out" the earlier chaotic family life including the beatings. As far as her father was concerned, he was a "grateful recovering alcoholic", who perhaps had made a few mistakes raising his kids, but in general, had been a great father! To make matters worse, his wife agreed. No wonder Kathy thought she was crazy, worthless and was having problems identifying with A.A. for her own alcoholism.

Kathy had stayed sober and had gone to A.A. meetings through all the turmoil, so she had that to build on. She got into a group of other ACoAs with stories of child abuse and pain "as bad as hers". This new family did not think she was crazy, although at first every time *she* disagreed or had a different opinion, *she* felt she was crazy and wanted to quit. The severe depressions and ideas about suicide stopped almost immediately because she was in a therapeutic setting that made sense to her and gave her a sense that there was indeed hope. In the group she learned to trust other people and talk about her feelings. She was able to try on new roles within the new family. She was able to take the interpersonal skills she learned in group and apply them to other groups such as her family, A.A. and work.

After two years, she not only got into a job which she likes and has been promoted at, but she is also getting married to a man who she loves and has been dating for over a year. She is well adjusted at work, at home and with her friend. She laughs about the fact that she used to think "I was a raving lunatic!"

"A.A. is Great — ACoA is Terrible"

There are a whole group of recovering people in A.A. who feel that anyone who brings up issues pertaining to growing up in an alcoholic family is a threat. They feel that these issues somehow undermine A.A. or are in competition with the principles of A.A. They feel that ACoA issues are a gimmick to bring people that aren't true 100% *bona fide* alcoholics into the A.A. program.

Since ACoA issues are psychological issues, and many recovering people in A.A. have been burned badly by psychologists, psychiatrists and other mental health professionals, there is a feeling among some recovering people that ACoA issues are baloney, or "trumped up" issues, which take the focus off the real problem — alcoholism.

While those feelings are quite understandable, the fact is that ACoA issues are real, and the price for denying them is also real. The truth is that many of the same people who get angry at anyone who would try to make A.A. more than "Just don't drink and go to meetings" by bringing up psychological issues or talking about underlying pain resulting from an ACoA childhood, are the very ones that are threatened by their own feelings. They stuff them, function "well enough" but pay a high price. If you grew up in an alcoholic family, you have to straighten out the distorted learning and emotional confusion that came out of that up-bringing. There's no way around it. You must pay the price.

"There's no free lunch!" as ex-President Gerald Ford said.

What is the price? Well, the price one man paid, who is an extremely successful public relations executive and has been in A.A. 12 years, is ulcers and chronic splitting headaches. He grew up in a terrible alcoholic family with a nice shiny middle class facade and is now in a constant rage because he never learned how to deal with anger within the family.

However, he can't ever show his anger, hates therapists and goes dutifully to daily A.A. meetings. "Everything was fine" in his alcoholic home, when it was not. And now that he is in A.A. and recovered everything is "again fine" — even though it is not. He looks twice his age.

Another recovering alcoholic female advertising executive with similar ACoA dynamics has developed an unexplained skin condition that causes her continuing pain and embarrassment. When people try to bury the large amount of pain and anger generated by growing up in an alcoholic family, those feelings often manifest themselves in their bodies. They "somatize" their feelings.

Another patient of mine was told by his A.A. sponsor to do "the fourth and fifth step" countless times. In other words he told him to take his own inventory of assets and defects, and also to go to church — to deal with overeating and depression resulting from the growing up in an alcoholic home. The result was that he got fatter and more depressed. He was basically misdiagnosed and maltreated by his own A.A. sponsor, who probably had untreated ACoA problems of his own.

Dry Drunks

Often, leaving these ACoA problems untreated, while ostensibly still working the A.A. program, results in feelings of depression, a constant low level bubbling of anger, rigid, inflexible opinions, acting out, either sexually or with physical violence, and other attitudes often associated with "stuffing" anger and pain. Most of the time, these "stuffed feelings" are the cause of what are called "dry drunks" in A.A. — where a person acts as though he were drinking, even though he has had no alcohol or pills.

Case in point, a hard driving "up-tight" but successful corporate lawyer suddenly bashed some stranger over the head with his umbrella because the stranger had splashed him with water from a puddle with his car. He knew his "little escapade" was not very sober, and he was embarrassed, but he really did not have a clue why he did it.

Dry drunks can go on for weeks. They can drive wives, husband, bosses and lovers crazy. They can be responsible for incalculable damage in terms of young children, when the "dry-drunk" verbally abuses them.

One six-year-old child who had just endured the uncontrolled name-calling of his father, who had been "sober" 10 years in A.A., was heard by his mom to say behind closed doors, "I want to kill myself — I want to not be here." That's a heavy price to pay for untreated ACoA issues.

Many times this "dry-drunk" syndrome goes away because the person throws himself into A.A. and works the program "extra hard". They go to extra A.A. meetings and "work the A.A. steps". But that is letting off steam. It is temporary, and more steam is gradually building up — because the real cause of the symptoms remains untreated.

The real cause is that the person never learned how to deal with emotion, including anger and pain, in an alcoholic family where feelings were denied. They cannot express them so they "stuff" them. The solution is that they have to learn to understand and accept those feelings and then to express them in an appropriate way.

In our culture, breaking through the denial on the second disease of co-dependency and learning to deal with your feelings is especially difficult for men.

There is a myth around that men are not supposed to show their feelings or they will not be considered strong. They are not "real men". To say how you really feel at the job, be it as a truck driver or a corporate lawyer, is asking to "get your butt kicked". To be emotionally open with your wife or with your buddies is to leave your flanks open. It is to "ask for trouble". Unfortunately this leads to a lot of "pretend tough guys" with ulcers, headaches and fat guts. It seems to me that there has to be some re-education that says that real men are those who are strong enough to cry and brave enough to face the pain of growing up in an alcoholic home.

What To Do

The most important fact to realize is that there are two separate diseases with denial systems — alcohol and co-dependency. A.A. only addresses, and only claims to address, the issues arising from alcoholism. On the one hand, some of those "tough guy old-timers" in A.A. are right. "Only matters concerning booze belong at an A.A. meeting — this isn't group therapy!" Or another way of putting it is that other problems concerning work or love should be talked about only in relation to their impact on drinking at A.A. meetings. Long emotional discussions about your latest "relationship problem" or your "family problems at age five" are out of place at A.A. meetings if they do not directly pertain to your feelings about drinking. These psychological problems are not appropriate for A.A. meetings.

However, they are real problems. They more than likely arise from growing up in an alcoholic family, and you have the right for them to be addressed. The proper forum where these issues should be addressed is with people who know something about them, such as ACoA or Al-Anon groups or with knowledgeable professionals. More about what works in dealing with these issues will be investigated in detail in the last chapter.

The most important thing is not to see mental health professionals who are aware of alcohol and co-dependency issues as enemies. Their insight and skills are often needed to deal with the complex psychological aspects of the second disease. Many of the mistakes made in the past by professionals are being remedied through education. In addition, great advances in terms of knowledge about alcoholic family systems and new therapies to address ACoA issues have been made in the last five years. There is nothing in any of the theory or practice of therapy that addresses ACoA issues that is antithetical or, even vaguely hostile, to the principles of A.A. Recovery from alcoholism and co-dependency are complementary.

But, I reiterate, "You don't take penicillin for cancer or chemotherapy for a cold." You do not go to A.A. for ACoA issues. It doesn't work. For those who have used the A.A. program of recovery to effectively deal with their alcoholism, a day at a time, and stayed sober, they deserve help for their second disease. After all, they did not get sober to feel like a piece of garbage. They deserve to get their boat "unstuck" and get effective help.

_____ **Chapter Five** _____

Can't See the Forest for the Trees

There are a myriad of Adult Children of Alcoholics who know that they are not alcoholic themselves, know that they are from an alcoholic family system, know that they need professional help to solve their emotional problems and *still* do not get the proper professional treatment. The problem is that they go to supposedly qualified therapists — psychiatrists, psychologists, social workers or lay analysts — who do not fully understand alcoholic family systems.

The ACoAs make some progress in therapy but basically never resolve their main conflicts, feel hopeless and then blame themselves. This is because the therapy situation replicates their original family situation where no matter how hard they tried, or no matter what they did, things did not change for the better. They often either quietly stay in therapy and never confront their therapist because of their need to be a "good patient" (just like they needed to be a "good child" in their family or origin), or they switch therapists and go through the same cycle again. In their hearts, they feel either that therapy does not work or that they have the kind of problems which are not solvable in therapy.

Sometimes they even feel they are genuinely "crazy" because often that is what it feels like to live in an alcoholic family where "up is down", "everything is just fine" when it is not "fine", and "denial" permeates everything. Sometimes, such as in the case illustration in this chapter, therapists hypothesize the wrong diagnosis or label a patient with mistaken and sometimes damaging labels — because they do not understand the whole picture. The patient's behavior is run through an inadequate diagnostic grid and comes out looking like something it is not.

The therapist fails to see the alcoholic family system from which the patient comes in its total context. In addition, he often does not understand what alcoholism is and how it affects different members of a family. He focuses merely on the dynamics of the individual. You might say, "He can't see the forest for the trees." In looking at the problems a patient presents, he looks at only one aspect of the system.

For instance, if a young woman comes in depressed because of problems with her boyfriend, the therapist spends the sessions looking at the dynamics between the woman and her boyfriend. Or he may explore her feelings, conscious and unconscious, about the first "big man" in her life — her father. That's fine as far as it goes, but what never gets mentioned is her functional role within her alcoholic family system, her father's relationship to her mother, or the impact of alcohol on the whole system. That is just a start! Without any of this relevant material brought to bear on the problem, an adequate diagnosis of the problem is impossible. What emerges instead is a limited, lopsided view of the problem that leaves many unexplained symptoms, behavioral questions unanswered and often obscures the real issues.

Worst of all, there is no realistic treatment plan for the patient. In my experience, when the total picture is seen and the emotional reality of the childhood experience is taken into account, most ACoAs' behavior and the problems they have make sense. If the ACoA begins to get an understanding and acceptance of themselves, then they have the option of changing that behavior. Without the analytic grid of the alcoholic family system, the patient's problems never get fully addressed in a realistic way. If looked at from merely an individual perspective, ACoAs are doomed to get "stuck" in therapy.

The best analogy I can think of is the poem about the six blind men and the elephant. Because they were blind, when asked what an elephant looked like, one grabbed its trunk and said "an elephant is like a snake," the other touched its side and said "an elephant is like a wall," and so on. The point is that they wind up with the wrong diagnosis!

ACoA issues are psychological, so they are often complex, subtle and do not lend themselves to a black-and-white solution as was the case with alcoholism. Often the resolution of the present predicaments and pain lies buried in the distorted attitudes and hurt feelings experienced in childhood. ACoAs are professionals at using words to cover up those painful feelings and telling other people, including therapists, what they want to hear.

In the following case, the problem is what is *not* being addressed, rather than a doctor pushing a certain viewpoint on the patient. Whether ignorance or maliciousness is the cause is beside the point. They all "miss the boat" at the patient's expense.

Elizabeth

Elizabeth is a 34-year-old attractive single woman from Boston who is working on her doctoral thesis in art history. She is an only child from an alcoholic family where her mother, Eloise, is the alcoholic and has been in recovery for about 20 years. However, she has not gone to A.A. regularly for about 10 years and has infrequent periodic "slips". Her father, Brad, is a highly successful banker from an "old Boston family", and is very influential around the city.

Elizabeth lives alone in an apartment that her parents pay for while she is finishing her thesis at a prestigious university in the area. She was self-referred to me because she was very depressed. She was "stuck" in therapy as well as with her work. She just had no energy to complete her thesis. She was also hopelessly in love with a professor who was married and who had said that he would not leave his wife and family for her. Having been in and out of therapy since she was 15, she had been seeing her latest therapist, a traditional psychiatrist, once or twice a week for three and one half years but she felt she was getting more depressed.

After taking the MAO inhibitors for over a year and a half, she had given them up a few months before coming to me. She also, on her own, and against her parents' advice, had started six months before to go to ACoA self-help meetings which she found extremely helpful.

Along with Elizabeth, I received a very recent psychological evaluation done by a certified clinical psychologist based on an interview with the patient, the Wechsler Adult Intelligence Scale-Revised Test, a Rorschach Test, a Thematic Apperception Test, a Beck Inventory Test, a Symptom Check Life — 90 Test and the reports of two different psychiatrists Elizabeth had seen for extended lengths of time. She had been to the same clinical psychologist nine years previously for a similar evaluation. Here is a summary of the results of the current evaluation.

The clinical psychologist felt she had deteriorated clinically during the nine years and regressed particularly in the areas of anxiety and depression. "She tends to blame herself." The several relationships she had with inaccessible or rejecting males had the cumulative effect of rendering her "utterly withdrawn and incapable of working. They triggered serious depressions with suicidal thoughts, feelings of hopelessness, nothing to look forward to and unbearable physical anxiety." He says she has become increasingly disorganized and there was no guarantee that she would not "crack under pressure".

The evaluation focuses attention on the increased anxiety and depression in terms of the rejection and maltreatment experienced by Elizabeth in relationship to her latest boyfriend. The resulting serious disorganizing depression is considered the main symptomatic component of her condition, but based on her responses to the Rorschach, he feels she may be somewhat cyclothymic — that's manic as well as depressive. Her increased withdrawal, negativism and suspiciousness are seen as an accentuation of the schizoid component of her personality. He notes that she was not enthusiastic about taking the tests and says there are "hints" of delusional thinking and paranoid "bents", but they are balanced by an active imagination and interest in the arts.

The Thematic Apperception Test shows that there is a "remoteness, a schizoid sort of separation of herself from her family. Mother never comes into clear focus . . . she is always looking away . . . possibly out of depression and anger." Her mother appears as a manipulator of both her and her father. This, the psychologist feels, colors her relationships to men, because she feels she has to anticipate and manipulate men as a means of protection against their manipulation. By the way, the

Wechsler Test showed that Elizabeth had an over 150 I.Q.

The summary suggests that Elizabeth has, according to DSM-III, which is the diagnostic manual for clinicians, the following diagnosis:

AXIS I: Cyclothymic Disorder (301.13)
AXIS II: Schizotypal Personality Disorder (301.22)

He feels the major affective attribute is that of depression but there are hypomanic elements intermingled. He concludes that "the patient is basically resistive and avoidant of a joint exploration in depth of her current psychological problems. This presents a significant risk, because it is possible that without greater participation in therapy, she may need hospitalization."

In the whole of the seven-page report the *only* reference made to alcoholism was, and I quote in its totality,

"Elizabeth's mother *had* been a long-term alcoholic, in treatment with Elizabeth's first psychiatrist."

Before looking at this case from a systemic perspective that includes the role of the disease of alcohol on the whole family, I think it is important to hear what all those years of confusion and therapy felt like from Elizabeth's viewpoint.

"I've been going to psychiatrists since my sophomore year in high school when Mom first got sober. She wanted to make sure I was not an alcoholic, for which the doctor reassured her. I was sad and isolated in high school but got great marks anyway and got into a first-rate college. During college I saw the clinic therapist for one session because of trouble with my boyfriend. He told me I was anhedonic — I love the word because it sounds like it's out of a Greek tragedy — which means against pleasure. Great!

"All during my master's degree, for almost three years, I went regularly twice a week to see my mother's psychiatrist, who supposedly was an expert in alcoholism. We talked about my problems with my current boyfriend and about how much I was bored with graduate school. He was very passive and said "uh-huh" a lot. We never talked once during the whole time about alcoholism and the role it played in my family. He knew my mother was an alcoholic because he had treated her, but I wasn't an alcoholic, so it never was brought into *my* therapy. The whole time I felt 'What am I doing wrong . . . with my boyfriend, with my career, with my therapy? I'm not getting any better!'

"But I didn't say anything because he was the doctor and I figured it was my fault. I stopped therapy after I got my master's degree, and got a job in a gallery in New York City. It was a short happy period lasting only a few years, in which I felt some measure of self-esteem and independence. I was developing some expertise in my field. I even got a new boyfriend. Then when I lost my boyfriend, I got depressed.

"I flew back up to Boston to see Mom's shrink again for about six months once a week. We talked about my feelings of abandonment because of this guy dumping me. Nothing ever got resolved, and I felt he gave me no directions or guidelines. Issues of trust and judgment were taken up without any reference to my alcoholic family. He said I should be more 'assertive' — that was the extent of it. As I look back, it was just a place to go and bitch! But I still could not understand why it didn't work out, why I had no new understanding and why I never felt any better. I figured it was my lot in life, and once again, I stopped therapy.

"I was generally mixed-up, but I continued to work for another year or so. Then I got into an argument with the gallery owner. It was a strike of sorts. I'm not sure whose fault it was, but it escalated rather quickly. All of the 'peons' in the gallery protested because we felt we were underpaid while he was making millions. But he felt otherwise and fired us all. Dad asked why I didn't come back up to Boston and get my doctorate. He offered to pay and also give me an apartment in Back Bay.

"Well, I went back to Boston and back to school. I floated around classes and did okay, but I spent more and more time hanging around my apartment. Dad, through his connections, got me a job in a Newbury Street art gallery, but after a year or so I lost interest and quit. So back to the halls of academy I went. I even got a topic for my thesis on Rubens. I decided to 'go for Baroque', so to speak!

"During this period I got mixed up with a married professor in the biology department, by the name of Emil. He was great looking, super-smart, but very closed about his feelings. He never really said he would leave his wife and kids for me. I really was madly in love with him, but felt I was not good enough. On the other hand, I would get angry at him for not paying enough attention to me.

"Anyway, I went to another psychiatrist, this time twice a week, to discuss my problems with Emil. I continued to work at my own pace on my thesis. That was three and one half years ago. She was a traditional M.D. shrink, a really nice lady, and a friend of my parents' friends. Mom got her for me. The new shrink basically said I had to get my act together and get a job for self-esteem.

" 'You need structure,' she would say. I translated that to mean that was all I deserved — a job, but no boys and no happiness! About Emil and me, all she said was that we were 'not intellectually compatible'. I don't think she understood how deeply I felt about him. I really loved this guy. She knew the history of alcoholism in my family, but it really never entered the therapy. Only once she said in reference to Emil, 'You feel abandoned because of your mother and her alcoholism. It's an infant issue.' She said it once, it made sense, but we never went back to it again.

"Then Emil stopped seeing me and I fell apart inside. I got depressed and started to obsess about him. I was getting worse and worse. She gave me tricyclics for my depression, but that did not work so then she put me on MAO inhibitors. I got euphoric. It was a real rush! I was hypomanic — working all the time and buying every-body gifts. I figured, so this is normal! I never knew what normal was because I'd been depressed for so long. Everything was great for about eight weeks. Then I gained 30 pounds, couldn't concentrate on anything and fell asleep at my desk. I was a mess!

"While on drugs, I don't remember what I talked to the doctor about. I was so drugged I didn't feel anything. I felt I was nothing. I suppose we talked about Emil because I was obsessed by him, but I really don't remember. I just knew I felt awful, and I knew I was getting worse. What I really could not understand was that I was doing everything she said and I still felt lousy. Underneath I felt gypped and angry but I said nothing. She said, 'You are every psychiatrist's dream patient because you do everything I say to do.' Now I couldn't even blame the shrink because she was so nice!

"It was during this period that the psychological evaluation was done. That depressed me more. She read me the report (the same one summarized in this chapter) and then I really felt there was no hope. The report, I felt, said I was one step away from being schizophrenic and was getting worse. I've never felt such despair in my life. Now I did feel suicidal.

"About this time, I saw a book in the Harvard Co-op by Judy Sexias and Geraldine Youcha on ACoAs called *Children of Alcoholism: A Survivor's Manual*. I read it at once and cried through the whole book. I felt hope for the first time. I got an appointment with my mom's psychiatrist who was the expert on alcoholism. He 'poo-pooed' the book and was very patronizing about the whole ACoA movement. I felt genuine fury in his office. I decided to do a little research on my own and sought a consultation with a therapist mentioned in the book. The ACoA consultant said that "one-on-one" therapy was not enough and that, in addition, I needed to go to ACoA self-help meetings several times a week in order to establish a network of friends — a surrogate family. I did that, and it helped. But when I told my own psychiatrist she said it was fine but really did not see it as significant.

"During this period I was at least able to get off the MAO inhibitors and I began to feel a bit better. But I still felt stuck. I couldn't get any work done on my thesis and I still obsessed about Emil. Every so often I would call him up. The sessions at her office seemed increasingly nonrelevant to my concerns. She finally admitted that she just did not know about alcoholic family systems. It was then that I quit and, through a friend in the ACoA meetings, got in contact with you."

Solving the Riddle

The real problem goes back to Elizabeth's alcoholic family system which is still actively functioning much the way it did when she was a child. I have news for you, Mr. Clinical Psychologist, Elizabeth's mother not *was* but *is still* an alcoholic. In fact, not even a very sober one. Although she does not actually drink very frequently, she doesn't go to many A.A. meetings. She still displays many of the characteristic attitudes of a drinking alcoholic. Elizabeth feels she is grandiose and narcissistic — the "center of the universe" syndrome. She does not listen now and never did listen to any of Elizabeth's feelings as a child. Then it was because she was absorbed in her drinking, and now it's because of her trips and houses and clothes. One could say it was like she was "facing in the other direction", thus, Elizabeth's accurate emotional response on the T.A.T. in the evaluation.

Her father was, and is, since he has never gone to therapy or involved himself in Al-Anon, a typical para-alcoholic, who is someone who stays married to an active alcoholic. His advice to his daughter was and still is to this day, "Don't upset Mom or she will drink." That translates as "Do not show anger or any negative feelings or your mother will drink and die. And it will be your fault."

Even the clinical psychologist notes that Elizabeth feels guilty and always blames herself — a chief characteristic of depression. Brad is scared to confront his wife for the same reason, and she "rules the roost". Who knows what goes on emotionally between Eloise and Brad — but one thing is for sure, they need a problem or a common cause to cement their bond. That cause is the same one that always kept them together — bringing up baby Elizabeth. Only Elizabeth is 34 years old.

For the sake of their marriage, they need to infantilize Elizabeth and do so daily. They are rich, and they never stop throwing money, clothes and apartments at Elizabeth. However, there are always strings attached. Nothing is ever given that is not tied to dependence on them. Apartments are owned by Brad, clothes are picked by Eloise and therapists also are picked by Eloise. Eloise's messages to her daughter are always, to this day, the same "you don't dress right", "you don't think right", and "what will you ever do without us". Brad chimes right in on that last one. They never stop telling Elizabeth how to run her life.

Elizabeth, as the only child in an alcoholic family, has the need, as she always did, to hold the family together at any cost and "not rock the boat". So Elizabeth stays crippled to fulfill her parents' unconscious needs. The cost is that she is furious — not anger but rage. However, since she can't "rock the boat or Mom will drink", she turns that rage on herself in the form of excruciating, sometimes even suicidal, depression.

The fact is that sometimes she would like to kill them but her role of the perfect little girl, or the perfect patient, won't allow her to even think about that. She just turns it back on to herself. Although the pattern for this way of dealing with anger lies in the past, the energy for the daily depression lies in the present — because her parents never leave her alone. They call her up every day, send her unasked-for presents and constantly ask "how she is doing?" They are manipulative, and they are always disguised — as benefactors. It is difficult to get angry at someone who is giving you something. Especially if you love and need them.

Suddenly all the symptoms start to make sense and the various issues fall into perspective. ACoAs are notorious for picking inaccessible partners. It is a replication of the way they got love growing up in an alcoholic family. Find someone who is lame or "not there" for you, try to be there for them and fix them up, then they will love you.

It's the syndrome so well documented in *Women Who Love Too Much* by Robin Norwood. Except, of course, it doesn't and never did work because you can't fix someone else. They have to fix themselves. But this explains Elizabeth's obsession with the various men. She was trying to get the love she never got at home, being unconsciously furious, and then turning that anger on herself and feeling inadequate and worthless. These men all reaffirm her low self-worth. It also explains why this is her first priority and she brings it into therapy all the time. What it does not explain is why the therapists did not recognize it for what it is and focus on the connections to her early home life, rather than waste years talking about her feelings about her boyfriends. They should have been much more directive.

The reason why Elizabeth gets depressed every time she sits down at her desk to do her thesis is because it is connected to her parents' constant nagging to get the thesis in so she can become a "doctor" and make them happy. Again, "her thing" has become an extension of their needs. She needs to get the thesis done. Yes, as psychiatrist #2 said, "She needs to get her act together" and needs "structure". However, she needs to feel that the thesis is hers, a passport to freedom from her parents by giving her the qualifications for a job which will guarantee financial as well as emotional independence. She needs to see all her problems in a context she can understand and do something about.

Elizabeth is not cyclothymic or nearly a schizophrenic. She is just plain furious with her mom and dad and with the mental health professionals who have been giving her the run-around for nearly 20 years — the same run-around she got at home, where she was supposed to get love and understanding, but instead got a deaf ear.

Elizabeth is not, as the psychological evaluation states, "resistant and avoidant of a joint exploration in depth of her current psychological problems." Quite to the contrary, she is cooperative, never misses a session and has a great sense of humor.

Since she has been in therapy, she has stopped calling and obsessing about Emil. She has started another relationship that, although far from perfect, is at least real. She talks about her feelings to this man, including her negative ones such as anger, and listens to what he says back.

Sometimes it is a bit "rocky" but she is taking it a day at a time. The emphasis in therapy is on deriving her self-worth from herself and not handing the power to define herself over to any other person — parent or lover. That power is hers alone!

For the first time in years, she has completed several chapters on her thesis. In fact, the famous professor who is overseeing her thesis asked her to co-author a book with him. It is a constant struggle to write the thesis, and she still gets depressed sometimes, but the emphasis in therapy has been that the thesis is a real way to combat her parents' smothering.

In the meantime, she has learned to say no to her parents' gifts if they are given with strings. She is not falling into their constant traps, even though they never stop trying. However, at least she knows she is angry, and that she has a right to be, even if she chooses not to express it.

In therapy, she is unlearning what she learned in her alcoholic family system — that you have no rights to feelings, especially anger. In point of fact, she has not really started any arguments or fights with them. She says her parents are quite happy with her. But inside she's learning to define her own boundaries — when to hold and when to fold. She's learning to see things in a new context. Best of all, she realizes that everything takes time and she has stopped beating herself up. For the first time in 20 years, she has hope.

_____ **Chapter Six** _____

Two to Tangle

Couples, in which one partner or both are ACoAs, often "miss the boat" together. Because they do not fully understand the "disease" concept, they misdiagnose what is wrong in the relationship and wind up maltreating each other and the relationship. They make the mistake of seeing the other person as the cause of the problems, label them "sick" and, of course, label themselves "healthy". Then they spend all their time blaming the other person, "analyzing" their faults and only sometimes telling them how they feel. Most of the time, the other person does the same thing.

The "he is the one with the problems, not me" posture is most obvious when one person is a drinking alcoholic, because alcoholics usually look worse on the surface than their partners. However, this game takes a more subtle form when one of the partners has an alcoholic parent and comes from a "mixed-up" family — which is always brought up when arguments arise. The non-ACoA partner's family is looked at by himself, and sometimes his mate, as "just fine". As we shall see in this chapter, in reality such is almost never the case. As we shall also see, couples form a system which must be kept in balance.

Aside from the misdiagnosis and maltreatment by members of the couple themselves, another problem comes up when the couple seeks professional help. Often professionals in the marriage counseling field are unaware of how to diagnose the alcoholism hidden within each partner's respective family system. And to make matters worse, they have no idea of how the alcoholism in each individual's family would influence the interaction between the couple. As we saw with individuals in previous chapters, much time is spent diagnosing and treating the wrong problem. Without all the pieces to the puzzle, the result is confusion.

"Problem" Relationship

Many ACoAs get into relationships with people that have "problems". Sometimes they even marry them. ACoAs are experts in trying to get love and nurturing by "fixing" people and their problems because that is what they learned growing up in their alcoholic families. The people with "problems" who they "fall in love with" usually come from dysfunctional family systems themselves, many times alcoholic family systems. In addition, "problem" partners may be alcoholic, even though the ACoAs swore to themselves that they would never become involved with an alcoholic or anyone from an alcoholic family.

How does this happen? The answer to this riddle of why ACoAs seem attracted to what they hate or know is no good for them lies with that old Sphinx — Pearl Bailey. As her song says and the chapter title alludes to, "It Takes Two To Tango". The individual partners in a relationship are each the product of complex multi-generational family systems containing a myriad of rules and beliefs, spoken and unspoken, conscious and unconscious, so that what one sees on the outside in a couple is like the tip of two "icebergs". Most of the relationship is under water. That is why the boat gets stuck. To understand the complicated dynamics *between* two "icebergs", when so many of the expectations and assumptions are below the surface, is difficult, to put it mildly. But, to understand certain basic principles of marriage counseling helps.

Problems in a relationship are never, repeat never, one person's fault. The truth is that all long-term relationships, including marriage, are equilibrium systems. Both people have to be willing to play the game or the relationship would fly apart. Even though it may fall apart and come back together many times, the very fact that the relationship stays together, presupposes that two people have found a certain equilibrium, albeit a turbulent one.

People almost invariably pick people of equal mental health — or lack thereof! No matter how "sick" one person may look on the outside or how "healthy, sane and saintly" the other person seems, the truth is that the "healthy" partner must have compensating emotional problems or unresolved issues to remain in the relationship. One might say, both partners' neuroses mesh, or as a friend of mine's Serbian grandmother said, "There's a lid for every pot." In my experience, no one who is "healthy" stays in long-term relationships with a "sick" person because he or she "loves him", "he'll die if I leave", or "for the kids". Those are merely excuses for not looking at one's own problems.

How It Works

People get into long-term relationships for both conscious and unconscious reasons. Often "chemistry" or "that special indefinable something" has more to do with the unconscious reasons. Simply put, what makes bad relationships is when people have unresolved emotional issues from childhood, like holes in a Swiss cheese, and they get involved with someone who they unconsciously expect to fill up the holes. Partner #1 projects onto partner #2 his own dream of partner #2. That projection has more to do with his own unresolved personal issues than it does with partner #2. Then partner #1 runs right smack into the reality of partner #2 instead of his projected version. He is then angry, frustrated and often tends to blame the other person for his own unhappiness. Partner #2 has holes in her own Swiss cheese and projects similarly — resulting in reciprocally blaming partner #1. And around it goes!

The reality is that no one can fill up anyone else's Swiss cheese holes. With help, each person has to fill them up him or herself. The more a person has the holes filled up, or never had the holes, the healthier the relationship will be. Remember, however, the system can never work if it is unbalanced for any length of time. The more each partner has his or her own individual act together, the better chance the relationship has to work because each individual does not need the other person to be fulfilled himself but is capable of giving and sharing because they want to — not because they have to.

Health in relationships is a continuum with needy, frustrated, "co-dependent" partners (dependent on each other to fill up the holes) at one end of the spectrum- expecting the impossible from their partner. At the other end are people with enough of their own issues resolved to see the partner realistically, accept them for who they are, with all their limitations, and still love them. In the middle lies reality — all of us — "just folks". I often point out to clients what a healthy relationship looks like. Though not real, it is at least a television couple we can identify with. It's not *Ozzie and Harriet* — but "Ralph and Alice". *The Honeymooners* are an example of a marriage that works. The Kramden's fight, cry and sometimes act foolishly, but they share their emotions, know each other's limitations, accept each other's foibles — and still love each other. "Alice, someday . . . to the moon!" is always followed at the end of each episode with "Honey, you're the greatest." They basically accept the holes in each others' Swiss cheese.

Most marriage counselors who have had clinical training in family systems theory understand what has been said so far in this chapter. It is basic marriage counseling theory. What they often fail to understand is the particular specific patterns that arise in alcoholic family systems and how they influence the interaction of people who are a product of these systems. In addition, marriage and family therapists who are not aware of the role alcohol plays in a family, fail to see the insidious tricks played by denial — both in regard to the alcoholism and the co-dependency.

ACoA Hook-Ups

The reason so many ACoAs hook-up with other ACoAs, including alcoholics, is that the pattern of holes in their Swiss cheeses, to push a metaphor, are often similar. In other words, they are all playing the game by the same co-dependent, mixed-up alcoholic system rules. They often take for granted the same basic crazy assumptions such as "you have no right to feel", "you have no right to express your emotions" or most of all, "don't ever trust" — because "up is down", "in is out" and "everything is fine" in an alcoholic family that operates on denial. Both partners often believe the same ACoA myths outlined by Janet Woititz in her book, *Struggle for Intimacy*, such as "We will never argue or criticize each other" — when in the real world couples argue from time to time, or "If I'm not in control at all times, there will be anarchy" — when in reality control has to be shared or even given up sometimes.

ACoAs often see the world in the same basic distorted perspective which comes from the particular emotional worldview of growing up in a denial saturated alcoholic family system. This often leads to false, unrealistic expectations of themselves, their partners and the relationship itself. They may fight with their partners, but they both know unconsciously that they are playing by the same unspoken rules.

ACoAs can also play the game with people from dysfunctional families where the hidden rules are similar to those in an alcoholic family system. These include families where at least one parent is a compulsive gambler, an overeater or chronically depressed. The main qualification for these dysfunctional families is that the parent refuses to get better and everyone in the family has to adjust to it. The rules to make the family function take on similar characteristics to alcoholic families. In all of these families, there is an absence of what normal is. There is also "denial".

People who grow up in these families have no idea of what healthy relationships are. Wherever would they learn them — on *"Ozzie and Harriet"*? They would not even recognize them if they saw them on *"The Honey-mooners"*. So the only ground rules or models for behavior that people from dysfunctional families have are ones that "don't work" — but at least the rules are familiar. They take these rules that don't work into new relationships and try to make them work in new dysfunctional relationships. The new dysfunctional relationships also provide an additional benefit for ACoAs and their partners. It allows ACoAs to play certain familiar roles, ones they spent their whole life learning, which although they may be painful, are at least known and therefore less scary.

People often underestimate how frightening it is to try new unknown behavior. For instance, if you were the "hero" in your "old" alcoholic family, trying to "fix" or "save" someone when they could not be "fixed" or "saved", it may be frustrating in your "new" family but at least you know how to feel inadequate, guilty and angry. If you've been a "scapegoat" in your alcoholic family of origin, it seems only natural to "act out" in your marriage by hitting or having an affair. If you've been used to the pain in your "old" alcoholic family by hiding in a "lost child" role, you'll have no trouble emotionally disappearing into a corner when your present partner pushes you around or emotionally ignores you. You've practiced the role daily since childhood. It is known territory. But if you are not that role deep within, then who are you? Maybe nobody! That is what is so frightening.

The same principle applies to marriage therapy when the couple understands a particular dysfunctional dynamic in the relationship and is forced to move to a higher level of health. They know what the problem is and must try to act differently. But they will often temporarily regress and "act out" at this point — pick a fight for no apparent reason because it is less scary to go back to the old behavior, which they both know is painful, than to try new behavior. If this resistance is pointed out, they can continue to make progress.

What complicates diagnosing the underlying interpersonal dynamics of an ACoA couple is the role played by denial. For instance, most alcoholics deny that they were alcoholics, and in the early stages of this progressive disease, the outward manifestation of their disease may be "invisible". It may be especially "invisible" to a person who is from an alcoholic family system who is still in denial about the alcoholism in his or her own family. Such ACoAs would never "marry an alcoholic" like their parent who is in a very advanced stage of the disease, but would never recognize the disease in an earlier stage in someone else. Daughters of male alcoholics and sons of female alcoholics are unconsciously attracted to alcoholic mates. They are "comfortable" trying to get nurturing from an alcoholic. But suddenly after years of marriage, they discover they've married an alcoholic.

If the ACoA is also a drinking alcoholic who hooks-up with another drinking alcoholic, then the whole relationship is really about booze rather than the other person at all. Romance and drama take the place of real intimacy. "Birds of a feather, flock together." Alcoholics like other alcoholics. They like to drink and fantasize together. Many great "lovers" are really drinking companions. Any counseling on a relationship such as this is less than worthless. *Both* partners must get sober first.

Thus there are all sorts of combinations for trouble for ACoAs in relationships. There is the

(1) ACoA-ACoA or dysfunctional family member hook-up
(2) the ACoA-active alcoholic hook-up
(3) the ACoA/active alcoholic-active alcoholic (probably ACoA but not necessarily) hook-up.

Rarely have I seen an untreated ACoA-nice healthy person hook-up! It doesn't make sense. Who's taking in the slack? The result of all these unconscious dynamics is a tangle which is often incomprehensible to the people caught in it. Thus it is important to look at real situations in order to unravel the tangles.

What follows are several cases: one couple consists of two alcoholic/ACoAs, another is two ACoAs, one of which is also an alcoholic, and the third example concerns an ACoA who keeps hooking-up with alcoholics. These couplings do not happen by chance but are the product of years spent living in alcoholic family systems. They also do not present themselves as what they really are. What you see is *not* what you get!

Peter and Betty

Peter's, age 28, and Betty's, age 27, courtship and five years of marriage had always been stormy. They yelled and screamed at each other daily and even hit each other once in a while — a regular Punch and Judy act! Ostensibly his anger revolved around his feeling that she was emotionally immature, irresponsible with the housework and by voicing rather directly some most unpopular opinions in a vocabulary usually reserved for the men's locker room. But she was his "little Betty" and he loved her. He put up with her.

She was furious because Peter always tried to patrol her as well as control her. She felt he was domineering, selfish and even at times a bully. But she loved his protection and "macho" quality. They had been to marriage counseling several times with absolutely no results. They both believed, at this time, that she came from a "screwed-up" family because her father was an alcoholic, but that his family was "just fine" — besides they were "classier" than hers.

. . . Until she realized as the result of one "outrageous" incident at a party, plus the caring of a good friend from childhood who was already in Alcoholics Anonymous, that she was an alcoholic. She got into therapy and A.A., and things began to look differently. She began to discover that his family was far from perfect. It began to look as though his mother was an alcoholic. In fact, Peter, on his own, began to question whether he might be an alcoholic. His brother was, most definitely.

From my vantage point, I could see that Peter's "taking care" of Betty was a version of taking care of his mother, who although not an "acting out" alcoholic was nevertheless an alcoholic who had always been emotionally dependent on Peter. She had always and still did confide in Peter about her "bad marriage". Peter could never make her happy and felt inadequate, guilty and in a rage like most "heroes" do. However, he never expressed any of these feelings to his mom, in fact, he was always "super polite" to her, but instead projected them onto "lame" Betty. He was always angry at Betty, *but* also attracted to her because she is an alcoholic — like Mom.

But Peter can't see she is an alcoholic because, as you might have guessed, Peter is an early stage alcoholic who is in denial. He is thus blind to his mother's, his wife's and his own alcoholism. Peter sedates all of the uncomfortable feelings coming out of this conflict with Betty and his mother, with alcohol. He never talks about his feelings. Sometimes the rage breaks through anyway, and Peter acts it out by screaming at or hitting Betty.

Betty, on the other hand, is attracted to Peter not only because he is big, strong and protective, but also because he's an emotionally unavailable alcoholic man — just like Pop! As the eldest girl, she spent her whole life trying to get her father to notice her. She was a super-achiever and brought home all sorts of accolades until her own alcoholism started to catch up with her. But he never did pay attention and still does not because he is preoccupied with his bottle.

So Betty has had the very best training available to try to accomplish this task with Peter. Of course, she could not accomplish it and was furious. She sedated those feelings of rage with alcohol, except when occasionally they would leap out like a jack-in-the-box. Now that she has stopped drinking, she must learn to deal with those feelings in A.A. and therapy. Previously, all the rules learned in their respective alcoholic family systems about not feeling, not talking, acting out rather than expressing anger, had been operative.

In addition, because they were two drinking alcoholics, drama and isolation substituted for expressing feelings or sharing. If the marriage is to work, her husband must break through the denial about his own alcoholism as well as his family's. He must get sober first, if any progress on the relationship is to be made. If it is to survive, the relationship, must remain relatively in balance. If marriage counseling is going to work at all, the denial issues must be dealt with first in order to provide a realistic framework in which to discuss the underlying ACoA psychological issues and develop realistic expectations for the marriage. At this point, after seven years they hardly know each other.

Christina and Don

Christina, aged 33, had come to me depressed about herself and her husband who was too busy with his successful law career, she felt, to pay attention to her. She did everything to please him, as a housewife and mother, yet he seemed preoccupied. She tended to blame herself and had spent time in therapy in the past talking about her mother, who was an alcoholic and had divorced her father for another man when she was a small girl. Her father, who she felt close to, was also a successful lawyer.

She was rather ashamed of her alcoholic family and her younger brother who was an angry rebel, had "busted" out of law school and probably had a drinking problem. Don, aged 35, who entered therapy at first to "help" Christina, came from a successful "healthy" Jewish family without any alcoholics. His younger brother, Bruce, had some problems, but he was finding himself at 31, and would eventually settle down to the legal profession.

The first thing in therapy to change was when Don admitted his increasingly large and secret Valium consumption. When he realized this and got into recovery, we began to take a look at his family. It was discovered that his 63-year-old father was an alcoholic who switched to pills after a "humiliating experience at a business conference" 30 years ago. It turns out that his grandfather was known as a "boozer", even though this fact was far overshadowed by the fact that he had founded one of Wall Street's biggest law firms. This means that his domineering mother's complaints about his indecisive father and her manipulative high expectations of Don were more than just "being a Jewish mother". Don, it came out in therapy, had the typical ACoA need to achieve to keep the family together and need to deny the unpleasant reality of the family's emotional life. His "caretaking" and "hero role" function in his family of origin were great practice for his new home with Christina. He could "help her out" like he did his whole family. He expressed his anger and frustration with Christina just like he did growing up — through distance and control. Add to that the increasing emotional distance caused by the pills used to sedate that anger and you have a realistic evaluation of Don's side of the marriage.

What emerged on Christina's side was that not only was her mother an alcoholic, but her father was also (the fact that Christina was not an alcoholic with those genetic odds is a minor miracle). So her depression not only stemmed from the anger at Don's overworking but also from the fact that he was becoming more and more emotionally inaccessible, and no matter what she did, it was not enough — just like Dad! She realized she was much angrier at Dad than she thought, and *not* just at Mom for leaving. With a complete picture of each person's family, why these two people hooked-up makes more sense. With the role of alcoholism in each person's family system factored in, some of the unrealistic expectations, unconscious needs and areas of possible conflict can be seen from a realistic perspective.

Judy and Chip

Judy is a 45-year-old corporate executive from an alcoholic home where her mother was the alcoholic. She has been divorced from her first husband, who is an active alcoholic, for 10 years. She shared an apartment with her 18-year-old daughter, who was presently away at college, who Judy felt might be an alcoholic. Since her divorce, she had been seriously involved with two other men, both of whom were alcoholic. She was presently involved with Chip, a 47-year-old investment banker, who was in a 17-year marriage to an alcoholic called Alice. He said he loved Judy but he just couldn't seem to leave the marriage because of his need to "save" his wife, who kept threatening suicide whenever he said he would leave. Besides, it would hurt his children. Judy got my name from a friend who had told her to go to Al-Anon for her daughter. Judy came to me to set up marriage counseling with Chip, who had agreed that they needed something and reluctantly consented. Judy knew, because of her own family and Chip's wife's alcoholism, that alcohol was part of the puzzle but she was not sure where it fit.

Judy could empathize with Chip because she had put up with alcoholics for years, i.e., her mother and first husband. She, like Chip, also always wanted to "help" or "save" them. In fact, this had been a bond in Judy and Chip's relationship. They both knew how miserable alcoholics could make you. Judy felt that she was always the caring, understanding one in a relationship, and she could understand Chip's need to be there for his wife *but* his inability to stick to his word was "driving her bananas".

For almost two years he had said he would leave Alice, and sometimes he did for short periods, but he kept going back. Sometimes he would lie and say he was away on business while secretly going back to his wife. He would "explain" it away, and she would believe him — for a while. But then it would happen again and again. She said she just couldn't take it. She had threatened to leave several times but could not make it stick. When I asked what happened when she told him she wanted to end the relationship, she told me he called her day and night (14 messages in one 24-hour period on her answering machine), swore his undying love and stood all night in the apartment house lobby to greet her with roses in the morning. She couldn't resist!

I said to myself, "That sounds alcoholic to me" — but I knew she would never know that because, having grown up in an alcoholic family, she had no idea of what normal was — even with an M.B.A.!

I asked her about Chip's parents, and she told me that his father, a successful businessman, had a drinking problem but that Chip didn't think that he was an alcoholic. I began to suspect that the reason Chip remained in his marriage for 17 years was not to "save" his wife but to "drink" with her. I told her I would like to see Chip before we started any marriage counseling.

Chip came to see me, and he was slick. But not that slick! After talking to him for one session, I realized that he was an alcoholic, but I also realized that because of denial he was not ready to hear that from me. I told him that because he was still married and had promised Judy to get a divorce before seeing her again, that he should work on himself and the commitment issue before we did any marriage counseling.

I refused to do couples counseling or to take him on as a patient. However, I gave him the name of a therapist who not only knew about marriage counseling, but also knew about alcohol. I knew he had to work on his own issues and alcoholism before he could look at the relationship. I sent him to someone else because I did not want him to confuse the two issues. He had to get sober for himself, not another person. He was disappointed and angry underneath, but quite compliant because he wanted Judy.

Judy, on the other hand, remained in therapy with me to work on her own ACoA issues including her relationship to her mom and dad, her daughter, the men in her life and the role of alcohol.

She is not seeing Chip for now, and is going to Al-Anon meetings. She participated in an intervention upon her daughter, who is now in recovery in A.A. She sees her relationship to Chip quite differently, and realizes he's an alcoholic. Chip is also in therapy, going to Al-Anon meetings — separate ones — and also learning to keep the focus on himself. Chip has even started going to A.A. meetings on his own.

They are both filling up the holes in their own Swiss cheeses. By keeping "first things first", they both have the first realistic chance to have a relationship and in the future there is now at least some possibility of marriage counseling.

Croon To The Moon By Yourself

Once properly diagnosed, the single most important ingredient in successful treatment for relationship issues is that both partners must define themselves as contributing to the problem and take responsibility for their own feelings. They must stop taking responsibility for the happiness of their partner, i.e., stop trying to "save them" or make them happy, and they must own up to the reality that they can only work on themselves. *In other words, both people must be in their own recovery!* When dealing with ACoA issues or alcoholism, one always has to take into account the role of denial. In a relationship, it unbalances the system.

The role of denial is especially important when dealing with relationships where one person is an alcoholic and has stopped drinking. The classic case is when one person returns from a month's visit to an inpatient alcohol treatment, and his or her spouse refuses to acknowledge the relationship has affected them as well. Often I hear from the non-alcoholic spouse, "They are the sick ones, there's nothing wrong with me!" The mate keeps blaming the recovering alcoholic, never acknowledging the change in him or her and absolutely refusing to see their own part in the "craziness" that went on before the alcoholic stopped drinking.

Nobody stays in a long term-relationship (without Al-Anon) with a drinking alcoholic who is not "crazy". Often the para-alcoholic mate will grudgingly acknowledge that at least the alcoholic has stopped drinking, but the para-alcoholic still maintains a resentful and punitive attitude toward the recovering person for "past sins". They usually refuse to go to Al-Anon or therapy or take part in the recovery.

One man married to a recently recovered alcoholic absolutely refused to see any connection between his outbursts of physical violence, his two previous alcoholic wives and his behavior in the present marriage. He saw himself as healthy. In his mind, he just had the bad luck to pick another "drunken loser". He spent 20 of his 42 years on earth living with alcoholic mates. People like this are usually angry when the alcoholic recovers because it tips the equilibrium of the system. They are in denial.

Spouses that stay married to alcoholics "enjoy" living with dependent people because — no matter what they look like — all drinking alcoholics are dependent people. Being on the other end of a relationship with an active alcoholic fulfills some unconscious need in them. At the very least, it keeps their minds off their own problems. When the alcoholic starts to get better, be less dependent and take care of himself, the spouse, without the help of Al-Anon and therapy, has a hard time adjusting. The system is out of balance.

What usually happens in a relationship like that is that either the alcoholic starts to drink again, thus putting the system back into equilibrium, or that the healthy partner continues to get better and outgrows the relationship and usually leaves. This is sometimes very painful for both partners, especially if there are children involved.

However, it is almost inevitable.

At first there are usually a lot of dramatics that replicate arguments that the couple had while the alcoholic was still drinking, but if the recovering person continues his therapy and A.A. meetings, he gradually loses interest in not only the old arguments but the old spouse. He finds her no longer exciting.

For example, a patient of mine who had been married 10 years and had two sons he loved, really had to make a choice. He had been recovered two years and had made great strides which were acknowledged by his business colleagues, his friends and reluctantly, even by his mom and dad. But his wife refused to see any change, blamed him for everything and absolutely refused to go to any therapy or self-help groups. Of course, she was 100 pounds overweight, and somehow, that was his fault also. Denial strikes again! After a period of several months of stormy arguments, another period of a few months of pleading and some false starts to get professional help, one more half year round of reasoning which always devolved back to arguing, he eventually lost interest and moved out. She finally went to Overeaters Anonymous (OA) and there was a happy ending to the story.

Another, more subtle form of denial takes place when one ACoA begins recovery for his co-dependent issues and the other person doesn't deal with their psychological issues resulting from their dysfunctional family of origin. Because of the various permutations of relationships that ACoAs can get themselves into, the forms of denial in a couple can get quite complicated.

I saw a couple who had been married 18 years, had teenage twin girls, and were both from alcoholic families. He was alcoholic and she was not. Six years ago he dealt with his denial about his alcoholism and went to A.A. However, he was still in denial about his ACoA issues. For a few years he stayed in A.A., and she got depressed. Then two years ago she started to go to Al-

Anon. Through Al-Anon and an in-patient program for ACoAs, she began to work through the denial about her ACoA issues. She became much less depressed and more angry. She became much more assertive about what she wanted emotionally from the relationship.

Her husband was still in denial about his second disease — co-dependency. He conformed to the type of person described in the chapter "Stuck". He could see he was an alcoholic but could not see any connection between his present emotional problems and his alcoholic family of origin. In fact, he felt he had no emotional problems. "Bad luck" had caused him to have four jobs in three years, and being "under pressure" had caused his periodic outbursts of rage at the twins. He refused to go to therapy for himself or for the relationship.

His wife stayed in therapy and to make a long story short, when the twins went off to college, she moved on to a career and another guy. In every case, where one person was in recovery and the other person was in denial, the relationship fell apart or regressed back to a less healthy and more painful state.

On the other hand, couples that do take responsibility for their disease usually grow together and are happy — no matter how bad it was when the alcoholic was drinking.

Sometimes, I have separated couples for up to six months after the alcoholic has returned from inpatient rehabilitation so that each partner can work on their own issues. During that period they lived separately and got together at first only on weekends for dates. They then gradually increased the amount of time that they saw each other, depending on their progress as individuals, as well as their progress as a couple. During this period, they worked on their own issues in individual therapy and went to the appropriate self-help groups. The distance from each other gave them a chance not only to look at their own issues but also to try on new, more flexible roles and to experience the other person differently. They tested out some of those hidden assumptions and expectations and processed their feelings in therapy or at self-help meetings.

When they resumed living together, more traditional joint marriage counseling sessions were necessary. However, the context of those sessions was usually very positive and the focus was on bargaining about real differences rather than blaming each other. [Of course, when there is stress on the family system from the outside, (for instance, a financial crisis or a family illness) we all tend to regress to our old ways. However, the difference in a healthy couple is that they have developed the individual and interpersonal skills to work their way out of those situations — progress rather than perfection.] In all cases, separating the couples, although it meant deferring short-term gratification for long-term goals, led to progress and eventual reunification of the couple on a more healthy, realistic basis. These couples all built new, healthy relationships.

In more traditional once-a-week couples therapy, the same truth reappears again and again — *when both partners take their individual programs of recovery seriously, then progress begins in the relationship.* One couple was in counseling for about six months and nothing was happening. He was from a "crazy" alcoholic family, and she was from an eccentric artistic family. It was only when she started in individual therapy and really began to see that her family was just as "sick", as his was, did real progress in joint session begin.

What To Do

Whether single, engaged or married — gay or straight — all relationships issues begin with you. *You can't change another human being. You can only change yourself.* Until you accept that premise, you are wasting time in any professional counseling. If you are already in couples counseling, stick to expressing only your own feelings, never assume you know what your partner wants or feels. And whatever you do, no matter how much you want to — don't blame — it's ultimately a waste of time.

If you are an ACoA or involved with an ACoA, or if you suspect your partner may be alcoholic or you yourself are recovered, make sure your marriage therapist knows about alcoholic family systems and how they interact. Otherwise, you are wasting your time and money.

If you enter any couples therapy, make sure you have, in addition, a program of your own. This may be individual therapy or a self-help program such as Alcoholics Anonymous, Debtors Anonymous or whatever program seems appropriate. The important thing is to acknowledge that you need help. Just make sure you don't walk into any professional's office thinking that there's nothing wrong with you — that it's your partner's fault! Because then you are wasting the therapist's time and your money. Keep the focus on yourself and listen to the music — because, as Pearl says, "It takes two to do the dance of love."

Chapter Seven

The Odyssey of Recovery

Like Ulysses sailing home from the Trojan War, your journey to recovery may be fraught with perils. Hopefully, so far in this book, we've explored some of the dangers and deceptions that wait unbeknownst to an unaware traveler — from "one-eyed therapists" to the "Scylla and Charybdis" of ignorance and denial. Even when one avoids the major perils, the journey to recovery is not always smooth sailing because there are sunny days and stormy days, that is part of life. However, the real issue is learning to sail.

Growing up in an alcoholic home is not a good place to learn how to sail, although the people there all say it was. You often wind up blaming yourself for getting "lost at sea". Like Homer's *Odyssey* itself, the journey of recovery is a journey of the self with a goal of finding a home which you've lost or have been away from. It is a recovery in the sense of finding, once again, the real talents, feelings and potential that have been covered over with denial and distortion — the scars of the family "Trojan" war — of growing up in an alcoholic family. It is a discovery in the sense of developing new ways to see things, new emotional skills for dealing with people and new feelings of trust and faith in the future.

Having explored many ways how people "get in trouble at sea" and what to avoid, it is only fair that I share what I believe to be, based on my experience as a therapist and an ACoA, the best guide to what works in sailing the "ship of recovery".

Before investigating what works, I feel that the prerequisite for working any program of recovery is a recognition of the importance of an inner or spiritual life. This is not necessarily a belief in organized religion and does not require a belief in any specific kind of God. However, it does require as a minimum, a realization that recovery is "an inside job" and that you can't control the Universe. Ulysses never made the mistake of thinking he controlled his own fate. He knew it was in the hands of the gods. That was his salvation.

What Works

Alcoholism

If you are an ACoA with two diseases — alcoholism and co-dependency — your primary disease, the one which must be addressed first, is alcoholism. What works in fighting alcoholism is Alcoholics Anonymous. Inpatient rehabilitation or some of the new outpatient rehabilitation programs are great for getting into A.A. Early recovery therapy groups or even in some cases individual psychotherapy that is alcohol-oriented are great for sticking with A.A. if a person is having trouble because of underlying psychological issues, such as those deriving from an ACoA background, which intrude into their early recovery. Such a person needs extra help. Inpatient rehabilitation programs are great for "repeaters", or ACoA alcoholics who have relapses and go back to drinking (or have "slips" as they say in the alcoholism field), in order to get them back into a program of recovery including A.A.

But, Alcoholics Anonymous must be the center of any program of recovery from alcoholism. Especially with the underlying emotional conflicts arising from growing up in an alcoholic family, any person who tries to beat alcoholism without A.A. is almost certain to drink again. They are basically foolish to try, and any mental health professional, no matter what his professional degree, who tells you otherwise, is also foolish.

Without the A.A. program of recovery, any alcoholic ACoA will be doomed to live an emotionally truncated life characterized by rigidity, stuffed feelings, especially anger, and the inability to have fun — "white-knuckling" life with a clenched fist. When the first big storm comes, they will not have any ballast in their ship, it will be tossed about like a cork on the sea, and eventually capsize.

All of the people that I treat who continue to make progress on ACoA issues, and who are alcoholics, also continue to "work the A.A. program" to a greater or lesser degree, depending on their individual needs and where they are in their recovery. This does not mean they go to A.A. every day for the rest of their lives, but it does mean that they never "outgrow" A.A. They realize that alcoholism can only be arrested "a day at a time" and that recovery from all the more complicated ACoA family and psychological issues rests upon the solid base of sobriety and abstinence from alcohol. Otherwise it is back to square one!

Co-dependency

Any kind of therapy or self-help program for dealing with issues arising from growing up in an alcoholic family must address the basic problems. There are many good books around describing the feelings experienced growing up in an alcoholic family, plus other books which talk about the various functional roles played by individuals within the alcoholic family system, or how the system as a whole functions. There is still a need to distill the essence of the damage done to the individual ACoA and to translate that into ingredients that must be included in any form of effective help for that damage. Let us look at the most crucial basic issues that arise from an ACoA background, and then look at their implications for getting help.

What Makes ACoAs Different From Other Dysfunctional Families?

No Trust

It is impossible to trust in a home where your alcoholic parent tells you that you are the joy of their life one day, *and then the next day,* for reasons you are not aware of, hits you or screams at you or your other parent or siblings. It is impossible to trust in a home where you see your drunken father make a fool of himself *and* the whole family but because of denial, says it did not happen. It is hard to trust other people if your father promises you something in a drunken blackout one day, *and then* swears that he did not promise it to you or gets mad at you the next day for asking.

After that, not only is it difficult to trust other people, but it is difficult to trust yourself. You begin to think that you misperceive things, or that you are a bad judge of character, or that you are "crazy". This kind of mistrust of others is very basic to who you are. You do not want to trust others for fear of being ridiculed, rejected or hurt in other ways. *So any help or therapy must establish an environment of trust.*

No Hope

It is difficult to believe things will get better if you have heard a thousand times all your life "I promise I'll stop drinking this time and things will get better," *and* it never does. It is difficult to have hope if your family growing up tried innumerable cures, anywhere from going to church to going to marriage counseling *and* none of them made any difference in the terrible quality of your home life because the real issue of alcoholism wasn't being addressed.

It is difficult to believe that change is possible if you tried your whole life to be a "good" student or a "good" athlete or a "good" son or daughter in hopes that your family would somehow change, *and* it did not change. It is particularly hard to have hope if you've been to two or three therapists and invested your time, money and done everything you could to be a "good" patient, *and* you don't feel any different.

You either think that you cannot change or that therapy does not work, even though you may try it one more time on the odd chance that it might work. But in your guts, you don't believe it will make any real difference. Why should you? Nothing in your experience would merit having faith. *So any form of help must give real hope for real change that can be experienced in the person's day-to-day life.*

No Feelings

It is difficult to feel things if you've been taught all your life not to feel things. Children in alcoholic homes are taught to not feel or to cover their feelings up.

"Daddy really hurt me when he screamed at me," is countered with "He didn't mean it," at least, or at worst, "It didn't happen."

All of Mom's constant high level of anger and over-reaction to mistakes children normally make growing up is explained away by the fact she has other problems (drunken Dad) or denial, by citing the fact that she is a "saint" or "doing the best she can".

You learn very early on in an alcoholic home that you are not entitled to have feelings. Your feelings do not count. You can't even have fun because it is just a matter of time before "the second shoe drops" and it's back to the same old crazy unpredictable game. Growing up in such an environment — why would you ever know you had feelings? And if you are vaguely aware you do have feelings, why would you ever feel you deserve to express them? On what basis has anything in the reality of your life taught you that you have the right to say what you feel? *So any form of help for ACoAs must focus on feelings.*

What Specific Ingredients In Therapy Address These ACoA Issues?

Trust

Since lack of the ability to trust is the number one issue, any therapeutic environment, whether inpatient ACoA rehabilitation program, outpatient aftercare, individual or ACoA self-help group must establish an atmosphere of trust. That means getting people to make a commitment to show up week after week, no matter what other things come up in their lives.

In one outpatient after-care group I've run for over two years, I replace anyone who drops out very cautiously. It's been basically the same seven people for the whole two years. In this group the changes were incredible! The group dynamics replicate a family so the participants have the right to expect it to be a healthy family. That means a family that is predictable, with the same people at the same time each week. If they are going to take a chance at putting out painful feelings, they have the right to expect that they can trust, not only that the people will be there but that those same people will know them well enough and grow to care about them enough to really understand them. They also have the right to trust that they will not get hurt. They must learn to trust that no one is going to "get them" when they put out uncomfortable or angry feelings or laugh at them when they put out things that they have always felt were "crazy" or shameful. There is so much shame around issues in an alcoholic family.

ACoAs in recovery must learn to let go of their shame. Thus a consistent, safe and tolerant atmosphere is the most effective means of building trust no matter what the particular modality of the help.

Hope

Hope, in the ACoA context, must be based on reality. ACoAs are used to lots of baloney. They've seen it sliced by professionals! In the therapeutic context, this means the therapist must know what he is doing, be positive and assertive, but not try to "save" the patient. The health, talents and other assets are naturally there in each damaged ACoA. They are covered by years of denial, defenses and distortions of reality.

In groups, when ACoAs see other people in the group

successfully work through issues they believed were
impossible to work through themselves, they start to
have hope based on real experience. In individual
therapy when a person tries doing something differently,
not just thinking or feeling it differently, and then sees
that it is a better way to do it, he or she begins to believe
in change. Things must make sense at the action level.
Any therapy that puts the main focus on ideas or feelings
that are not subsequently connected into action "misses
the boat". Therapists must show ACoA patients that
recovery works in their own lives. That it is not just talk.

I feel that therapists who deal with ACoAs must be
much more directive than with other patients. For
instance, in dealing with a woman who keeps going out
with alcoholic men, it is important to point out the price
she pays, rather than endlessly exploring her relationship
to her father or her boyfriend. Although exploration of
the relationship to her father has merit, it must be
applied to the action level — the level on which she runs
her life. ACoAs do not know what normal is, so often
they need direction.

Therapists that deal with ACoAs must not only know
the clinical information about alcoholism and alcoholic
family systems, but also they must know themselves.
They should be in some form of recovery themselves.
Otherwise it is difficult to stay honest with themselves.
It's difficult to expect honesty from patients if one's not
honest oneself.

I've found that sharing experiences from my own
ACoA background is extremely helpful to patients. I also
try to admit if I make mistakes, or if I am confused about
an issue. I say that I'm not perfect and do make mistakes.
That takes the pressure off a patient to be the good
"perfect" patient. If patients see that I am not some
idealized, aloof, "perfect" therapist, but another ACoA
who has worked through many ACoA issues myself, but
still has some to work on, then they can identify with me
and experience real hope that change is possible.

While I realize that it is not possible for all therapists to be ACoAs themselves, or even to come from dysfunctional backgrounds, I feel a necessary ingredient to successful therapy for ACoAs is for the therapist not to take an emotionally detached, aloof posture towards the patient.

Feelings

Any treatment for ACoAs must focus on getting in touch with and expressing feelings. "Awareness" or "insight" is not enough. Therapies which are limited to dreams, free association and talk, such as psychoanalysis, are relatively ineffective in dealing with ACoA issues. In fact, sometimes they can be harmful. ACoAs are masters at using words to cover feelings. They intellectualize and rationalize to hide from their anger and pain. The more educated and sophisticated they are, the more adept they are at playing the game. The "plug" of this particular ACoA resistance fits right into the "socket" of "talk therapies". As you've read in this book, patients can spend years getting no place at great expense — really short circuited!

Good ACoA therapy must contain an experiential component. That means some role-playing, family sculpture, or even the use, under supervision, of "ba-ta-ka bats". The experiential component is needed to ensure that the glacier of intellectual defenses is broken through. ACoAs must learn to experience their feelings. That does not mean that the experiential part is the only part. I feel it works best when combined with more traditional interpretive and educational techniques. Different forms of therapy use experiential techniques to different degrees, and different individual therapists also vary in their use of these techniques. However, the experiential ingredient is a "must" in the recipe.

Different Forms Of ACoA Help

Given these primary essential ingredients, effective help for ACoAs takes many forms which can be combined according to the needs of each individual ACoA. Each different modality, like a tool, has its particular use as well as its limitations. Depending upon your needs and at what point you are in your therapy, any of these tools can be used to help you on your journey to recovery. Recovery from co-dependency is a continuing process and not a "one-shot deal".

1. Inpatient ACoA Rehabilitation Programs

There are some excellent inpatient rehabilitation treatment programs that address the emotional issues of co-dependency or growing up in an alcoholic family system. Some of them last five days, some of them are eight days and a few are a month in duration. Some are family programs which are part of a program for the member of the family who is in a month long inpatient rehabilitation for alcoholism; in other words, a "family week" which is included in the alcoholism rehabilitation program. Some are more educational in nature, while others have a large experiential component. Again, the best ones do more than just "talk" about the problem.

In all of them, the ACoA patient goes and lives at the residential treatment facility for the course of the program. These programs are like icebreakers in terms of getting through the glaciers of resistance and denial that ACoAs have. They open up feelings. Often patients make big changes in their lives after participating in them. As opposed to inpatient programs dealing with alcoholism, ACoA inpatient treatment programs do not necessarily have to take place at the beginning of ACoA recovery. I sometimes send ACoAs who are already in outpatient groups or individual therapy, and who are "stuck" to these programs. The good ones are very effective, but they are not to be undertaken lightly, *and they are not to be undertaken without the follow-through of individual or group aftercare.* ACoAs who open up that Pandora's box of feelings often feel vulnerable, curious and confused when they emerge from that safe inpatient environment.

The intensity of many of the feelings opened up for the first time can feel overwhelming. Time is needed to digest those feelings. Time is needed to integrate those emotional insights and apply them to everyday life. That is where aftercare and self-help groups come in. That is where the real ongoing work begins.

2. Outpatient Group Therapy

Outpatient group therapy is not just aftercare for inpatient rehabilitation programs, in fact, many ACoAs never go to inpatient rehabilitation. It is a therapeutic modality all by itself. ACoA therapy groups replicate the family, thus, they are particularly helpful in regard to working through "old" family issues and applying them to present situations. As opposed to inpatient programs which "open-up" new feelings in ACoAs, outpatient therapy attempts to "integrate" those feelings and "apply" them to everyday life.

Like inpatient treatment, outpatient therapy has an important goal of keeping ACoAs in touch with their feelings. In fact, group therapy is often the only place where ACoAs, who are usually "performing" well in the outside world, feel safe to "feel". Thus, such experiential techniques of role playing and family sculpting are used to "get at" and "open up" the feelings and more traditional interpretive techniques are used to integrate and apply the feelings. Because of the weekly on-going format of out-patient group therapy, participants have an opportunity to apply the new skills "worked through" in therapy to the outside world.

These old dysfunctional ways of feeling and living do not go away if we talk about them once or twice in therapy. They are deeply ingrained ways of feeling that "that's the way the world really is", which were learned in the alcoholic family of origin day after day for decades. They cannot be "unlearned" in a few days. Change is a process that takes time.

"Time is God's way to prevent everything from happening all at once," a man with over 20 years' sobriety once pointed out to me. Issues must be talked about, then tested in the real world, then talked about again, tested again and so on. Often patients, when they try new patterns of action are "surprised". They expect one thing and, then when they test it out, something entirely different happens. Pow!

The "surprise" is the gap between their projection of the situation which is based on the emotional reality of their childhood experience and the reality of the present situation. Patients are time and time again "surprised" when they confront their boss at work about "what they are entitled to" and find out that he does not dismiss them or disregard their feelings the way their alcoholic fathers did.

The "surprises", in my experience, are usually of a positive nature. They can be used constructively by ACoAs if they are properly understood to help clear up emotional distortions from childhood and to take further risks of new healthy behavior — which are usually frightening. When the patient takes the new risks while in ongoing group therapy, they have the support of a group which not only cares but is also aware in some depth of the situation.

Many times patients have got through a "holiday" visit with their parents who are still drinking by role-playing the possible situations first in group therapy and then, if they need to, calling various members of the group for support during their visit home. Many ACoAs can get "unconfused" about the way they feel in a therapy role play before talking to their lover or boss. If they do not do it "right" the first time, they try again in the group.

Another technique which has proven very effective in outpatient group therapy is using the telephone with other members of the group. Often confusing or depressing situations are caused by projecting feelings from childhood onto the present situation. People isolate in the "iron bubble" of their projections and cannot see their own realistic options. It is then that they feel hopeless or depressed or "crazy". They are basically talking to themselves. It is like they are in a dark room bumping into furniture. That is very scary. It is at that exact moment that they need to "touch the wall", break out of their projection and get some bearings of what is real and what their real options for action are. That is only a phone call away if they can talk to another person in the therapy group or anyone who is healthy and they can trust.

This "using the telephone" is not to be confused with subgrouping or "forming special friends" within the groups, which I discourage and feel sabotages the therapy. Outpatient group therapy has its limits in dealing with particularly difficult issues, in which sometimes I suggest either inpatient rehabilitation or individual therapy. But, through the week-in week-out progress of group therapy, ACoAs not only reaffirm in some realistic way among peers the real internal changes they are making, but they also can affect changes in the outside world — change jobs, get married, reconcile with parents — and have a consistent "non-crazy" context in which to interpret those changes.

3. Outpatient Individual Therapy

Individual outpatient therapy is best used in conjunction with group therapy unless the ACoA has particular issues in terms of getting along with a group, such as schedules or geographical distance, which prevent group participation. Sometimes individual ACoAs start in individual therapy, and then move on to group therapy. Sometimes individual therapy, like a microscope, is used to "zero in" on particularly resistant issues in relationships or the workplace that first become apparent in a group session. Sometimes individuals can benefit from both individual and group to help their growth process. *It depends on the individual.*

The more I am a therapist, the more I have respect for the individual growth process of each person. I am reminded of an ancient Chinese saying that appeared in, of all places, Mao Tse-tung's *Red Book.* "The rice plant grows when it grows, and if the farmer goes out in the field and tries to makes it grow faster by tugging on it, he pulls it up and it dies." *Different ACoAs grow at different rates. Recovery is not a race.*

Individual therapy depends, more than most therapists would like to think, on the chemistry between therapist and client. However, in terms of treating ACoAs, a thorough knowledge of alcoholic systems is a prerequisite to having any individual therapy work. That also means a thorough knowledge of alcoholism.

4. Self Help Groups

Al-Anon and ACoA self-help groups are extremely helpful in recovery from the issues arising in an alcoholic family. The more the self-help groups conform to the ideal of being consistent, predictable, personable and trustworthy, the more they will be able to help the individual. Sometimes Al-Anon or sometimes ACoA meetings are more helpful in dealing with particular issues. It depends on the person and the issue they are struggling with. However, ACoA or Al-Anon meetings, where the same people show up week after week, and where the meeting is small enough so that people can get to know and trust each other, are particularly helpful.

Huge meetings where people, who are not even sure if they are ACoAs, come to "dump" problems about their latest relationship or their discovery that they are "angry people" are not helpful. In fact, sometimes they can be harmful because Al-Anon and ACoA groups are not therapy. There is no knowledgeable person or therapist in charge to prevent people from getting hurt.

For instance, they are not the best forum to talk about such issues as incest or child abuse. These issues often scare everyone, including the speaker, when brought up in an open speaker format. They are not the place to vent rage or to confront other members of the self-help group. There is no positive context to make sense out of such venting of emotion. There is no one there to make sense out of it in some consistent helpful way. It often undermines the very trust and hope that the meetings try to inculcate.

Self-help meetings are an excellent place to find support, build a network, break through isolation and learn about the "disease".

5. Conferences and Workshops

Conferences and workshops focusing on alcoholism and the family serve a very vital function in ACoA recovery in terms of introducing ACoAs to new information and experiences. They also serve to rejuvenate and update ACoAs at many points along the road to recovery. However, they are *not* a substitute for a day-to-day program of recovery. One may make major breakthroughs both emotionally or intellectually at a workshop that lasts a few days. However, follow-through is needed when one returns home in order to integrate and apply the new insights to one's everyday life.

Many sincere ACoAs who want to recover come back

full of enthusiasm and good intentions from a conference only to get depressed or disillusioned because they
do not plan some organized, coherent plan of recovery
for themselves. Without follow-through, it is a "set-up"
to feel that "all this ACoA hoopla" is just another fad and
has no more validity than the other mental health fads
that seem to gather a head of steam every few years in
our country. It is a "set-up" to feel just like one did in
one's alcoholic family system where real change was not
possible.

However, the many conferences are excellent for not
only education but also breaking isolation. You can
experience that you are not alone and also experience the
feelings of a growing ACoA community committed to
recovery.

The Possibility Of Real Change

Good ACoA therapy gives realistic hope, based on
trust of others and knowledge of yourself, that you *can*
change your life for the better. It gives you more options
not less. It strives for independence rather than dependence on any person or group. Its exploration of feelings
is focused on the goal of translating those new options,
based on self-knowledge, into action. The goal of ACoA
oriented therapy is the same as the goals articulated by
Dr. Sigmund Freud when asked for a one liner on the
purpose of therapy, which is "to make the unconscious
conscious". Whenever thoughts or feelings are unconscious, repressed or "stuffed" — they control us. If they
are conscious, then at least, we have the option to make
choices about how to run our lives.

Many ACoAs still ask the question deep down in their
hearts, "Is real change possible? Can I really live my life
day to day so I feel good?"

In my experience, both personally as an ACoA and

with the people I treat, recovery is not only possible, but in most cases probable. With the proper treatment, ACoAs go on to live productive and fulfilling lives. But it does not happen overnight.

As I said before — it takes time. As St. Augustine expresssed it over 1500 years ago: "Lord, make me perfect, but not yet." That bit of wisdom is often easy to forget.

Substantive change takes time. It happens in an hour on TV or three hours at the Opera or in just 15 minutes in a comic book. But in real life all change takes place in small ways — it is one step at a time. That is not just for ACoAs, but for everyone. What happens for many ACoAs is that they have such high expectations for themselves, in recovery as well as other areas of their lives, that when they don't measure up to these expectations, they feel "they are no place", "recovery can't work for them" or a variation of those feelings, and then they give up. And the recovery process stops.

It becomes a self-fulfilling prophecy which originally comes out of the projection of their early years in an alcoholic home, where there was no point in trying because things really would not change. At the first storm, these ACoAs "take down their sails and go home".

If ACoAs work a recovery program which includes some of the five different modalities of help listed in this chapter, then they do change. No one can tell me otherwise because I've seen a young businessman, who was suicidal and utterly without hope, dig into therapy and a recovery program and two years later get married, get promoted at work and, more importantly, be happy with his life. I've seen a young woman with an alcoholic father who felt that she was destined to date alcoholic and often abusive men, finally find a healthy, good-looking man who she loved and who loved her — she did not "settle for less" — after spending the time in therapy addressing her ACoA issues. And I've seen a married couple who, after 27 years of bickering over alcoholic issues, finally settle down to get to know and enjoy each other — after they had worked on these issues. In fact, my experience is that the vast majority of ACoAs who get the proper treatment and do not get discouraged and quit, do get better. Honest!

If there is any message to this book it is one of hope — realistic hope! The message is that real change, based on proper diagnosis and treatment, is an exciting adventure. I, and no other person or program, cannot promise that the journey to recovery will always be "smooth sailing", but I can convey my firm belief in the validity of sailing itself as a worthwhile way to travel, my enthusiasm for the trip, and my recommendation that if you are an ACoA, you not "miss the boat".

But don't take my word for it, let's go to the symbolic heart of the American dream and take the word of the most famous child of an alcoholic in American literature — Huckleberry Finn — as he floats down the Mississippi River in his journey to freedom from his alcoholic father, who has just threatened to kill him with a knife in a drunken rage.

"I didn't lose no time. The next minute I was a-spinning downstream soft, but quick, in the shade of a bank. I made two mile and a half, and then struck out a quarter of a mile or more toward the middle of the river, because pretty soon I would be passing the ferry, and people might see me and hail me. I got out among the driftwood, and then laid down in the bottom of the canoe and let her float. I laid there, and had a good rest and smoke out of my pipe, looking at the sky; not a cloud in it. The sky looks ever so deep when you lay on your back in the moonshine; I never knowed it before."[5]

Amen, Huck!

---

[5]Mark Twain, *Huckleberry Finn* (New York: Harper & Row, 1948), p. 48.

Epilogue

The problems presented in this book, which are caused by ignorance and denial on the part of both professionals and the general public about the disease of alcoholism and its impact on the American family, can be realistically attacked through education. There is a great need for the sharing of information and for communication about already existing resources, as well as the development of new ones, between people who are concerned with families in the mental health field (be they psychiatrists, psychologists or social workers) and alcoholism professionals.

To put it briefly, the people who are already sophisticated about family systems must learn about alcoholism, and the people who are knowledgeable about recovery from alcoholism must become more sophisticated about how families function.

In the past because these two groups of treatment providers developed independently, they become isolated from each other. They evolved from different theoretical bases, worked in different kinds of institutions, used different sources of funding, read different publications and, thus, saw the world very differently. In terms of networking, family therapists belong to such organizations as AAMFT (American Association of Marriage and Family Therapists), the APA (American Psychological Association), the AMA (American Medical Association) or the AFT (American Family Therapy Association). People who work in the field of alcoholism belong to the Association of Labor-Management Administrators and Consultants on Alcoholism (ALMACA), the National Association of Alcoholism and Drug Abuse Counselors (NAADAC), the National Association of Children of Alcoholics (NACoA) and such self-help groups as Alcoholics Anonymous, Al-Anon, and Adult Children of Alcoholics.

The two groups of associations hardly knew of the existence of one another, let alone talked to each other. A major result of such such independent and isolated development has been ignorance; ignorance about the resources and knowledge that were available and would help their own clients.

Fortunately, all of this is changing for the better. There is a growing awareness among the professionals in the field of alcoholism that it is a "family disease", which affects not only the "alcoholic" but his or her whole family. Everyone in the family needs treatment. As more family treatment programs are developed, the recognition of the need for a more thorough knowledge of family dynamics is also being recognized.

Similarly, among mental health professionals, the reality of how pervasive, destructive and "hidden" the disease of alcoholism is among the people they treat, is becoming more and more apparent. The media has made the public, including family therapists, much more aware of of drunk driving and of alcoholism as a disease. In addition, because of the changes that are going on in the health care system across the country, many individual therapists and developing group practices want to work in private industry — where the majority of problems handled by Employees Assistance Programs (E.A.P.) involve alcohol and drugs. Thus, many previously uninformed professionals are beginning to see that it is in their best interest to become knowledgeable about alcoholism and the family.

There are a number of joint national and regional conferences being planned by the organizations in each group, as well as new courses on alcoholism and the family being developed for education by organizations from both "camps". Cross-fertilization is beginning to happen.

The primary issue is still education. The more people in each professional community learn about each other and the impact of alcoholism on the family, the more they will realize how much they have all "missed the boat" on a problem which directly affects one out of three families and is as much a part of America as apple pie — or at least Huckleberry Finn.

_____ **Appendix I** _____

Controlled Drugs

Benzodiazepines

WARNING: Giving a recovering alcoholic one of the following is like giving him or her a drink of alcohol. These drugs are a hazard to his/her sobriety and health.

Chemical or Technical Designation	Drug Company Trade Name
Alprazolam	Xanax
Chlordiazepoxide	Librium
Clobazam	Frisium
Clonazepam	Clonopin
Clorazepate	Tranxene, Azene
Diazepam	Valium
Flurazepam	Dalmane
Halazepam	Paxipam
Lorazepam	Ativan
Midazolam	Versed
Nitrazepam	Mogadon
Oxazepam	Serax
Prazepam	Centrax, Verstram
Temazepam	Restoril
Triazolam	Halcion

Schedules of Controlled Drugs

The following have been classified as addictive or potentially addictive:

Schedule I: (All nonresearch use forbidden.)

Narcotics: Heroin and many nonmarketed synthetic narcotics
Hallucinogens:
  LSD
  MDA, STP, DMT, DET, mescaline, peyote, bufotenine, ibogaine, psilocybin, phencyclidine (PCP) (veterinary drug only)
Marihuana, tetrahydrocannabinol
Methaqualone

Schedule II: (No telephone prescriptions, no refills.)

Narcotics:
  Opium
  Opium alkaloids and derived phenanthrene alkaloids: Morphine, codeine, hydromorphone (Dilaudid), oxymorphone (Numorphan), oxycodone (dihydrohydroxycodeinonone, a component of Percodan, Percocet, Tylox)
  Designated synthetic drugs: Meperidine (Demerol), methadone, levorphanol (Levo-Dromoran), fentanyl (Sublimaze), alphaprodine (Nisentil), sufentanil (Sufenta)
Stimulants:
  Coca leaves and cocaine
  Amphetamine (Benzedrine)
  Amphetamine complex (Biphetamine)
  Dextroamphetamine (Dexedrine)
  Methamphetamine (Desoxyn)
  Phenmetrazine (Preludin)
  Methylphenidate (Ritalin)
  Above in mixtures with other controlled or uncontrolled drugs
Depressants:
  Amobarbital (Amytal)
  Pentobarbital (Nembutal)
  Secobarbital (Seconal)
  Mixtures of above (eg, Tuinal)

Schedule III: (Prescription must be written after 6 months or 5 refills.)

Narcotics: The following opiates in combination with one or more active non-narcotic ingredients, provided the amount does not exceed that shown:

Codeine and dihydrocodeine: Not to exceed 1800 mg/dL or 90 mg/tablet or other dose unit

Dihydrocodeinone (hydrocodone and in Hycodan): Not to exceed 300 mg/dL or 15 mg/tablet

Opium: 500 mg/dL or 25 mg/5 mL or other dosage unit (paregoric)

Stimulants:

Benzphetamine (Didrex)

Phendimetrazine (Plegine)

Depressants:

Schedule II barbiturates in mixtures with noncontrolled drugs or in suppository dose form

Aprobarbital (Alurate)

Butabarbital (Butisol)

Glutehimide (Doriden)

Taibutal (Lotusate)

Thiamylal (Surital)

Thiopental (Pentothal)

Schedule IV: (Prescription must be rewritten after 6 months or 5 refills; differs from Schedule III in penalties for illegal possession.)

Narcotics:

Pentazocine (Talwin)

Propoxyphene (Darvon)

Stimulants:

Diethylpropion (Tenuate)

Mazindol (Sanorex)

Phentermine (Lonamin)

Fenfluramine (Pondimin)

Pemoline (Cylert)

Depressants:

Benzodiazepines:

Alprazolam (Xanax)

Chlordiazepoxide (Librium)

Clonazepam (Clonopin)

Clorazepate (Tranxene)

Diazepam (Valium)

Flurazepam (Dalmane)

Halazepam (Paxipam)

       Lorazepam (Ativan)
       Oxazepam (Serax)
       Prazepam (Centrax)
       Temazepam (Restoril)
       Triazolam (Halcion)
    Chloral hydrate
    Ethchlorvynol (Placidyl)
    Ethinamate (Valmid)
    Meprobamate (Equanil, Miltown, etc.)
    Mephobarbital (Mebaral)
    Methohexital (Brevital)
    Methyprylon (Noludar)
    Paraldehyde
    Phenobarbital

Schedule V: (As any other [non-narcotic] prescription drug may also be dispensed without prescription unless additional state regulations apply.)

Narcotics:
    Diphenoxylate (not more than 2.5 mg and not less than 0.025 mg of atropine per dosage unit, as in Lomotil)
    Loperamide (Imodium)

The following drugs in combination with other active, non-narcotic ingredients and provided the amount per 100 mL or 100 g does not exceed that shown:

Codeine: 200 mg
Dihydrocodeine: 100 mg

-------- **Appendix II** --------

Resources

Excellent sources of information are no further away than your telephone book. Usually located under Alcoholism in the yellow pages (sometimes under Drug Services). These sources include local Alcoholic Anonymous, Al-Anon and Adult Children of Alcoholic groups.

* Employee Assistance Programs are offered through the individual's company

* Military Treatment Centers are worldwide for active duty personnel

* Veterans Administration Hospitals are available for former service personnel

Head Offices for Information and Referrals

* Al-Anon, Al-Anon Adult
  Children of Alcoholics
  and Alateen Family
  Groups
  Box 862
  Midtown Station
  New York, NY 10018-086

* Alcoholics Anonymous
  Box 459 Grand Central
  Station
  New York, NY 10163

° Adult Children of Alcoholics
Box 35623
Los Angeles, CA 90035

° Batterers Anonymous
Box 29
Redlands, CA 92373

° Debtors Anonymous
Box 20322
New York, NY 10025-9992

° Divorce Anonymous
Box 5313
Chicago, IL 60680

° Emotions Anonymous
Box 4245
St. Paul, MN 55104

° Families Anonymous
Box 344
Torrance, CA 90501

° Families in Action
Suite 300
3845 North Druid Hills Road
Decatur, GA 30033

° Gamanon
Box 967
Radio City Station
New York, NY 10019

° Gamblers Anonymous
Box 17173
Los Angeles, CA 90017

° Incest Survivors Anonymous
Box 5613
Long Beach, CA 90805

° Nar-Anon Family Groups
350 5th Street, Suite 207
San Pedro, CA 90731

° Narcotics Anonymous
Box 9999
Van Nuys, CA 91409

° National Single Parent
Coalition
10 West 23 Street
New York, NY 10010

° Overeaters Anonymous
4025 Spenser Street,
Suite 203
Torrance, CA 90503

° Parents Anonymous
22330 Hawthorne Boulevard
Torrance, CA 90505

° Parents Without Partners
7910 Woodmont Avenue
Washington, DC 20014

° Pill-Anon Family Programs
Box 120 Gracie Station
New York, NY 10028

° Pills Anonymous
Box 473 Ansonia Station
New York, NY 10023

° Prison Families Anonymous
134 Jackson Street
Hempstead, NY 11550

° Single Dad's Hotline
Box 4842
Scottsdale, AZ 85258

° Survivors Network
18653 Ventura Boulevard,
#143
Tarzana, CA 91356

Publications

CHANGES for Adult Children of
Alcoholics
1721 Blount Road
Pompano Beach, FL 33069
Subscription: 1 year — $18.00

COA Review
The Newsletter About Children
of Alcoholics
P.O. Box 190
Rutherford, NJ 07070

FOCUS on Chemically
Dependent Families
1721 Blount Road
Pompano Beach, FL 33069
Subscription: 1 year — $22.00